Praying
the Lord's
Prayer

Praying *the* Lord's Prayer

AN AGELESS PRAYER FOR TODAY

Herman C. Waetjen

TRINITY PRESS INTERNATIONAL
Harrisburg, Pennsylvania

Trinity Press International, P.O. Box 1321, Harrisburg, PA 17105
Trinity Press International is a division of the Morehouse Group

Library of Congress Cataloging-in-Publication Data

Waetjen, Herman C.
    Praying the Lord's Prayer / Herman C. Waetjen.
       p.   cm.
    Includes bibliographical references.
    ISBN 1-56338-276-8 (pbk. : alk. paper)
    1. Lord's prayer – Criticism, interpretation, etc. I. Title.
BV230.W24 1999
226.9′6077 – dc21   99-25004

Printed in the United States of America

99 00 01 02 03 04   10 9 8 7 6 5 4 3 2 1

To
Extraordinary friends!

Joan and Carl Basore
Wendell Butler
Inger and Frank Hewitt
Mary and Bill Langford
Betty Obata
Sandy and Royce Truex

Contents

Preface

According to John 14:13, Jesus said, "And whatever you should ask in my name, this I will do, so that the Father is glorified in the Son." An astonishing, open-ended promise! Yet how often have we experienced its fulfillment in the prayers and intercessions we have offered to God in the name of Jesus?

But the promise is connected to the asseveration of John 14:12 by the conjunction "and":

> Amen, amen, I say to you, the one who believes in me will do the works which I do, and greater [works] than these she or he will do because I am going to the Father. And whatever you should ask in my name, this I will do, so that the Father is glorified in the Son.

In other words, whatever we should ask for in prayer must have some relationship to the activities we engage in, but specifically those activities that correspond to the works of Jesus as they are recounted in the Gospel of John.

Accordingly, the subject matter of prayer is open-ended yet conditional. Jesus promises to do whatever we ask, but what we ask for in prayer must conform to the kinds of endeavors and undertakings that are attributed to Jesus in the Fourth Gospel. This is prayer that is fully responsible for what is being said, for what is being asked for. The works attributed to Jesus are formidable, to say the least, and daring to engage in comparable activities presupposes a disposition toward extraordinary possibility that is willing, like Martha in John 11:39–40, to believe in order to see. To conceive of engaging in comparable activities, not to mention doing even greater works than those of Jesus, requires a fundamental reorientation to the reality of possibility that is absent from the empirically oriented culture into which we have been socialized, a five-hundred-year-old culture in which truth has been based on and limited to the experience of our five senses. The prerequisite is the fulfillment in us of the prayer that the deutero-Pauline author of Ephesians offers on behalf of the Ephesian Christians:

> that the God of our Lord Jesus Christ, the Father of glory, give you the spirit of wisdom and of revelation in the knowledge of God, having the eyes of your hearts enlightened so that you may know what is the hope of his calling, what is the wealth of the glory of his inheritance among the saints, and what is the immeasurable greatness of his power in us who believe according to the working of his great might which he accomplished in Christ. (Eph. 1:17–20a)

What, then, is the subject matter of prayer? What should we pray for in the light of Jesus' promise, "whatever you ask in my name, I will do it"?

Prayer has been characterized as the deepest and most completely free cry from the heart. Such prayer is natural, spontaneous, unpremeditated, evoked from within us by intense emotional experiences. Those cries of the heart may be articulate responses to occurrences of ecstasy or despair, good fortune or suffering, life-threatening danger or sickness. They may also be wordless sighs and groans, and they may not even be addressed to God. Nevertheless, God's Spirit, who dwells within us, intercedes for us; and God, who knows the mind of the Spirit, comprehends our thoughts by decoding these sighs and groans (Rom. 8:26–27).

The content of spontaneous, unpremeditated prayer tends to be subjective. It may include significant others in our lives: family members, relatives, friends, and even circumscribed groups to which we belong. But as right and valid and meaningful as such prayer is, it is incomplete. Its horizon is generally limited to our immediate world of personal affairs and relationships. Larger issues of justice and peace, poverty and homelessness, moral and environmental crises are usually ignored or omitted.

Perhaps that is why the apostle Paul said, "We do not know what is fitting for us to pray." Perhaps that is also why Jesus instructed his disciples to pray what has traditionally been called the Lord's Prayer. He offers guidance in praying about those realities in which God is also involved, issues in which God is actively interested and engaged. These are the actualization of God's rule on earth and therefore also the fulfillment of God's will, and not the least the veneration of God as Creator and Redeemer. This socially oriented content prompted Walter Rauschenbusch to characterize the Lord's Prayer as the "great prayer of social Christianity." In *Prayers of Social Awakening* he wrote, "its deepest significance for the individual is revealed only when he dedicates his personality to the vaster purposes of the kingdom of God, and approaches all his personal problems from that point of view. Then he enters into the real meaning of the Lord's Prayer, and into the spirit of the Lord himself."[1]

The Lord's Prayer comprehends this subject matter, but from the distinctive perspective of Creator-creature relationships that result from the death and resurrection of Jesus of Nazareth. At the same time the Lord's Prayer includes personal matters, such as daily bread, forgiveness of sins, liberation from guilt, and deliverance from the ordeal of being tested and tried.

Prayer presupposes a relationship with God, and without that relationship prayer has no value. Attendantly, prayer is worthless if the person praying is not fully responsible for what he or she is saying. These are the principal issues that this study of the Lord's Prayer attempts to elucidate:

---

1. Walter Rauschenbusch, *Prayers of Social Awakening* (Boston: Pilgrim, 1901), 16–17. My thanks to Hampton Deck, the pastor of the First Presbyterian Church of Vallejo, California, for lending me this stimulating book. Rauschenbusch's social Christianity did not affect his androcentric language.

1. Who are we before God? What is the nature of our rela-
    tionship with God according to the earliest witnesses of New
    Testament Christianity? How does the apostle Paul, the only
    representative of the first generation of the Christian move-
    ment in the New Testament, understand Christian identity on
    the basis of the death and resurrection of Jesus Christ?

2. Do the Gospels of Luke and Matthew, in which the two
    versions of the Lord's Prayer are transmitted, convey a cor-
    responding sense of Christian self-understanding in their
    presentations of the Good News of Jesus Christ?

3. What meaning might the individual petitions of the Lord's
    Prayer have for those who pray it consciously with a discern-
    ment of whom they are addressing and therefore who they
    are before God?

The elucidation of these issues will lead to a more inti-
mate and energizing relationship with God and therefore a
meaningful and responsible praying of the Lord's Prayer.

The introduction presents the two ancient versions of
the prayer and proposes a search for a frame of reference
in order to make its individual petitions more immediately
transparent in meaning. The first chapter, entitled "Who Are
We Before God?" according to the apostle Paul, may seem
out of place. Although there is no hint of knowledge of the
Lord's Prayer in his letters, Paul has formulated a theological perspective of Christian self-understanding that can serve
as a frame of reference for a vital and responsible praying
of the Lord's Prayer. Additionally, in Galatians 4:6 and Romans 8:15, contexts in which he expounds on the essence
of Christian identity, Paul employs the Aramaic word for father, *Abba*, the title Jesus used when he addressed God and
therefore the form of address that he taught his disciples. At
the conclusion of this chapter I would want to say to the
reader: "On the basis of this Pauline orientation, pray the
Lord's Prayer."

I would extend that invitation to include the following
chapters on the Gospels according to Matthew and Luke.

Pray the prayer Jesus taught his disciples in these narrative worlds on the basis of the foundational self-understanding that these Gospels convey. Each petition of the Lord's Prayer becomes more immediately transparent in relation to their perspectives of the Christian faith and Christian identity.

The two versions of the Lord's Prayer are subsequently interpreted, petition by petition, in the light of the foundational frame of reference that is derived from these Gospels and that was presupposed, I am convinced, for the praying of the Lord's Prayer at the beginning of the Christian movement. That will be as effective in uttering this prayer in this time as it must have been in antiquity. The translation of the individual petitions are my own, based on the twenty-sixth edition of the *Novum Testamentum Graece* edited by Kurt Aland and Barbara Aland.

An epilogue has been added at the recommendation of my friend and former student Douglas K. Huneke, pastor of the Westminster Presbyterian Church in Tiburon, California. It gives voice to the meanings that this study of the Lord's Prayer has generated for me. At the end I risk offering a revision of the prayer that employs fresh language in an effort to make its ancient content more transparent to those who no longer understand it and find themselves praying it by rote. I am grateful to him for this prompting as well as for various other changes he proposed.

A glossary of terms defines certain words that have been employed in the chapters, words that belong to the jargon of the academic world of theological seminaries and schools of divinity.

I have received much-needed criticism from many friends and members of my family who have taken the time to read an early draft of this manuscript. Dr. Sandra Brown of San Francisco Theological Seminary has been a searching critic, challenging me repeatedly with questions of meaning when I have been content to use biblical terminology. I have been the beneficiary of exchanges with another friend and former student, Chandler Stokes, pastor of the First Presbyterian Church in San Anselmo and New Testament scholar, on all chapters of this book, and from time to time I have adopted some of his pertinent phraseology. Inger Hewitt and Royce Truex, among the "extraordinary friends" to whom this book is dedicated, have read that early draft and responded with both affirmation and alarm. In the light of their critique I have altered many a word and phrase, inserted sectional headings in each chapter, and added the glossary of terms. My son, David, confronted me with the necessity of keeping my interpretive efforts as simple as possible and adding certain words to the glossary, but especially the urgency of elucidating the phrase "frame of reference" that is central to my effort to make the Lord's Prayer more intelligible. I am grateful to my daughters, Thembisa and Elaine, for their sustaining interest and support. To my wife, Mary, I owe an incalculable debt of gratitude for her inspiration and affirmation, and particularly for her tireless reading and rereading of the drafts through which this manuscript has evolved.

Finally, I am especially indebted to Dr. Harold W. Rast for his thoughtful and expeditious supervision of this manuscript and to the staff of Trinity Press International for their meticulous care and superlative editorial work.

I thank all of them profoundly for their tireless encouragement as well as for their grace in constructive criticism, all of which contributed significantly to the improvement of the content and character of this book.

HERMAN C. WAETJEN

September 6, 1998
Beginning of Christian Education Week

Praying *the* Lord's Prayer

The Lord's Prayer and a Frame of Reference for the Interpretation of Its Petitions

Two versions of the Lord's Prayer were handed down in the first century of the Christian movement. Both of them are preserved in the New Testament: one in the Gospel according to Matthew, generally dated around 85 C.E.; the other in the Gospel according to Luke, which may have been composed between 90 and 100 C.E.[1]

The Versions of the Prayer

The Matthean formulation is the longer of the two, and it is the version that has been most widely used in both public worship and personal piety in the subsequent history of the Christian church.

> Our Father, the One in heaven!
> Your name be held in awe;
> Your rule come;
> Your will come to be, as in heaven also on earth;
> The bread for our existence give us today;
> And forgive us our debts as we also have forgiven our debtors;

---

1. C.E. (of the common era) and B.C.E. (before the common era) are being generally used in place of A.D. and B.C.

3

> And do not bring us into a test,
> But deliver us from the wicked one. (Matt. 6:9–13)[2]

The Lucan rendering is shorter and very likely also earlier:

> Father!
> Your name be held in awe;
> Your rule come;
> The bread for our existence keep on giving us each day;
> And forgive us our sins,
> For we also forgive everyone owing us;
> And do not bring us into a test. (Luke 11:2–4)

Of these two traditions, the Lucan version may be the original formulation, even though the Gospel in which it is preserved was composed ten to twenty years after that of Matthew. Characteristically traditions in their early stages of formation, in contrast to their subsequent development, tend to be meager and lean. As they are transmitted from one context to another and from one generation to another, they are modified and amplified according to cultural circumstances and ideological orientations. Accordingly, Matthew's rendering of the Lord's Prayer is an elaboration of the simpler version preserved in Luke's Gospel. Not only does it contain the latter in its entirety, but also its expansions are extensions of the Lucan formulation of the prayer that probably developed in the liturgical context of Matthew's community.

A version of the Lord's Prayer is also preserved in the *Didache*, an early second-century instruction manual on Christian morals and church order.

> Our Father, the One in heaven!
> Your name be held in awe;
> Your rule come;
> Your will come to be as in heaven also on earth;
> The bread for our existence give us today,
> And forgive us our debt as we also forgive our debtors;

---

2. The translations that are offered for the Matthean, Lucan, and *Didache* versions of the Lord's Prayer, as crude as they may seem, are literal translations of the Greek texts.

And do not bring us into a test,
But deliver us from the wicked one;
For yours is the power and the glory forever [literally, into
    the ages].

Although the superscription of the *Didache* claims that
the content of the manual is the "teaching of the Lord"
transmitted by "the twelve apostles," its version of the
Lord's Prayer corresponds to Matthew's formulation almost
word for word. The differences are minor except for the
attribution that has been attached to the prayer and that
subsequently has become universalized as its doxology: "for
yours is the power and the glory forever."[3]

Because of its dependence on Matthew's formulation, the
Lord's Prayer in the *Didache* cannot be regarded as an in-
dependent tradition. Only the separate versions in Matthew
6:9–13 and Luke 11:2–4 appear to have been circulating in
earliest Christianity. In the course of time the closure of the
Lord's Prayer that was appended to the *Didache* was added
to the Matthean version, and that combination eventually became the predominant tradition in the liturgy of the church.
The Lucan composition of the prayer, however, is the earlier version, perhaps even attributable to Jesus as its author,
according to the witness of both Gospels. Its authenticity
as his formulation may never be established with any final
certainty. But that is not the critical problem of the Lord's
Prayer. Paramount is the matter of its interpretation. What is
the meaning of its content, the so-called seven petitions?

Human activities, like praying, generally have a context
in which their relevance and meaningfulness are established.
Teaching, for example, is always related to a particular subject matter and usually is done in a classroom. Doctoring has
to do with medicine and is performed in a hospital, a clinic,
or a physician's office. The context of both activities involves
a conjunction of subject matter and location. Beyond that,

---

3. See chapter 10 for more about this doxology.

there is a foundational perspective or a philosophical viewpoint that serves as a frame of reference for these activities. Teaching may be determined by a particular psychology of education. Teaching English, or any language, may be governed by a theory of linguistics. Practicing medicine will be shaped by the latest research and proven methods of diagnosis and treatment.

Analogously, praying the Lord's Prayer belongs to the activity of prayer, and its context is the liturgy of public worship in a church building or personal devotion in a private setting. Beyond that, there is an underlying theological perspective or foundational viewpoint, a frame of reference that determines the self-understanding of those who participate in the activity of praying.

Praying in general and praying the Lord's Prayer in particular may be done in congregational worship or in private devotion. The theological perspective or frame of reference that underlies and governs this activity in those settings varies from denomination to denomination and from Christian to Christian. But the critical question is to what extent that foundational viewpoint, whatever it may be, promotes the activity of praying in a meaningful way. More specifically, to what extent does that frame of reference promote the comprehensibility of the Lord's Prayer by making its content more transparent?

Is there a perspective beyond denominational differences by which the activity of praying can be carried on in a more consequential way? Is there a more universal frame of reference by which the Lord's Prayer can be prayed more intelligently, more responsibly?

Searching for a Frame of Reference

Many prayers that are spoken in a service of worship have stipulated references that inform and determine their meaning. A pertinent example is a Jewish prayer in which the content explicitly refers to the Day of Atonement on which it is prayed and by which it becomes meaningful:

> Our God and God of our fathers, pardon our transgressions on this Day of Atonement; remove our guilt, and blot out our iniquities, as Thou hast promised:
>
>> "I, even I, blot out thine iniquities for My sake, and thy sins will I remember no more. I have made thy sins to vanish like a cloud, and thy transgressions, like a mist; return to Me for I have redeemed thee. On this day shall ye be forgiven and cleansed from all your sins; before God ye shall be pure."
>
> Praised be Thou, O Lord, who forgivest transgressions, King of the world, who sanctifiest Israel, and the Day of Atonement. Amen.[4]

Similarly, a Christian prayer that names the liturgical context in which it is to be prayed poses no difficulty in apprehending its meaning.

> May our experience of Christmas be real, O God,
> Not just something to observe, but a life to celebrate!
> Keep uppermost in our thoughts
> The great gift of your son to us
> So that the commercial trappings of Christmas
> Do not overwhelm us.
> Send us forward from Christmas
> To share your gift of love with others. Amen.[5]

Prayers that imply a liturgical setting in which they are to be prayed may also be transparent in their meaning. An example is a Jewish prayer that is spoken on Rosh Hashanah at the "Evening Service for the New Year." The content of the prayer, particularly the use of the second person imperative in its individual petitions entreating God for safekeeping, is unambiguously meaningful in its context.

---

4. *The Union Prayerbook for Jewish Worship*, rev. ed. (Cincinnati: The Central Conference of American Rabbis, 1948), 342.

5. Sarah Klos, *Prayers Alone/Together* (Philadelphia: Fortress, 1970), 27.

Cause us, O Lord our God, to lie down each night in peace, and to awaken each morning to renewed life and strength. Spread over us the tabernacle of Thy peace. Help us to order our lives by Thy counsel, and lead us in the paths of righteousness. Be Thou a shield about us, protecting us from hate and war, from pestilence and sorrow. Curb Thou also within us the inclination to do evil, and shelter us beneath the shadow of Thy wings. Guard our going out and our coming in unto life and peace from this time forth and forevermore. Amen.[6]

A Christian example is a prayer for a funeral or memorial service. Although no setting is named, its use in an Order for Burial enables an effortless comprehension of its meaning.

Father, your love is stronger than death:
by you we are all being brought to life.
Help us, as we hear your promises,
to believe them and receive the comfort they offer.
You are the giver of hope:
fill us with joy and peace in believing,
so that we may have abundant hope through the power of
    the Holy Spirit.
Glory to you, our God, forever. Amen.[7]

The Lord's Prayer, however, stipulates no liturgical context in which it is to be prayed and by which its content might be illuminated. A few of its petitions are immediately transparent: "Give us today our daily bread," "Forgive us our trespasses, as we forgive those who trespass against us," and perhaps "Deliver us from evil." But the remaining petitions are not so obvious in their meaning, and nothing in the liturgical context of worship mediates a comprehension of their subject matter. No immediately accessible interpretive key seems to be at hand for the elucidation of this ancient prayer.

It seems necessary, therefore, to venture back to the be-

---

6. *The Union Prayerbook,* 16.
7. Klos, *Prayers Alone/Together,* 105.

ginnings of the Christian movement and specifically to those Gospel texts that have preserved the Lord's Prayer in order to search for a theological viewpoint, a frame of reference, that will make the content of Jesus' prayer more intelligible. Such a foundational perspective may enrich and intensify the general activity of praying.

The Matthean Context of the Lord's Prayer

The immediate literary setting of the Lord's Prayer in Matthew's Gospel offers nothing that might make its content as a whole more transparent. No faith perspective accompanies the teaching of the prayer that might make the meaning of its petitions self-evident. Jesus, after warning his disciples not to babble or be wordy in their praying because "your Father knows of which things you have need before you ask him," commands them to "pray thus" and proceeds to teach them his formulated prayer (6:7–13). At the conclusion of the prayer, before he moves to the subject of fasting, he emphasizes the point of the fifth petition:

> For if you forgive human beings their trespasses, your heavenly Father will also forgive yours; and if you do not forgive human beings, neither will your Father forgive your trespasses. (6:14–15)

Nothing of this instruction elucidates the content of the Lord's Prayer. It is necessary, therefore, to examine the Gospel of Matthew in its entirety in order to recover a frame of reference that is presupposed for the intelligent praying of the prayer. More specifically, the theological-spiritual perspective that it presents and the self-understanding that emerges from that perspective will generate a more meaningful and responsible praying of the Lord's Prayer.

The Lucan Context of the Lord's Prayer

In Luke's Gospel the prayer is located in a context of Jesus engaging in the activity of praying:

> And it happened as he was in a certain place praying, as he paused, one of his disciples said to him, "Lord, teach us to pray, even as John taught his disciples." He said to them, "When you pray say...." (11:1–2a)

At the conclusion of the prayer Jesus proceeds to tell the story of the guest at midnight:

> Who of you will have a friend, and he will come to him in the middle of the night and say to him, "Friend, lend me three loaves of bread, because my friend came to me from the road, and I do not have anything which I might set before him." That one inside might say, "Don't bother me! The door is already locked, and my children are in bed with me. I'm not able to rise and give to you." I say to you, "Even if he will not rise and give to him because he is his friend, he will rise and give him as much as he needs because of his shamelessness."
> (11:5–8)

Such an event was probably typical of village life in Palestine. Guests might arrive unexpectedly in the middle of the night; and the unprepared host was obliged to offer hospitality. If he did not have the resources, he was dependent on his fellow villagers, his neighbors, to alleviate his embarrassment and help him to set food before his guest. Jesus' introductory question "Who of you...?" would lead his hearers into making a judgment about the motivation of the neighbor who finally gets out of bed in order to assist the host in entertaining his guest — not because of the mutuality of friendship but because of the individual's shameless behavior. Jesus himself steps into the story at the decisive moment when it appears that the host will be frustrated in his efforts to receive the food he needs for his guest. "I tell you," he declares, "even if he will not rise and give to him because he is his friend, he will rise and give him as much as he needs because of his shamelessness."

The perplexing word here is "shamelessness" *(anaideia)* or "being without shame." In a society determined by honor/shame culture, such as the Mediterranean world of the first century, shamelessness is a negative value.[8] But to whom in this story is it to be attributed? To the petitioner, the one asking for bread? Or the petitioned, the one who does not want to get out of bed in order to respond to the request for three loaves of bread? The question may be answered by determining the identification of the ambiguous pronouns of the story:

He will not arise and give *him* because *he* is *his* friend.

He will arise and give *him* [as much as *he* needs] because of *his* shamelessness.

The one in bed will not arise and give the petitioner bread because the petitioner is the petitioned's friend. Friendship, as surprising as this may be to contemporary readers, is not the primary motivation to fulfill the petitioner's request. It is rather his shamelessness, his loss of self-control and the resulting dishonorable conduct in an honor/shame culture. For his rude and aggressive behavior in the middle of the night is driven by his desperation to secure bread for his unexpected guest. The circumstances of time and the urgency of his need have overwhelmed his reliance on the mutuality of friendship.

In first-century Mediterranean culture, friendship was based on reciprocity, the mutual give and take of material goods and services. Shamelessness, in whatever way it was expressed — rudeness, effrontery, impudence, brazen-

---

8. In so-called western society, in which Americans participate, the word "shame" and the reality to which it refers is negative. Shame is a feeling that I experience when I have done something that is considered to be dishonorable or improper in the society in which I live. However, "shame" in an honor/shame culture is a positive value. A person has shame when she or he acts honorably in accordance with the values of honor/shame culture.

ness, boldness — was dishonorable conduct and therefore could only evoke a negative response. Yet as negatively as shamelessness was regarded, it was ironically the behavior by which the petitioner's objective was achieved. However it expressed itself, as audacity or presumption, unmannerly intrusion or indiscretion, it arose out of his desperate condition of "I have nothing."

Metaphorically Jesus' story places his disciples and God in the context of village life, and the relationship between them analogously is that of neighborhood friends. God is parallel to the individual who is behind a locked door and already in bed; the disciples, whom Jesus has taught the Lord's Prayer, are represented by the friend knocking at the door and requesting three loaves of bread. Like the person already in bed, God will respond to them but not simply on the basis of friendship, which was dependent on reciprocity. God will give them all they need because of their shameless desperation. Their frantic and impetuous cry, "I have nothing," as outrageous and disrespectful as it may be, evokes God's response. God acts in freedom and not according to the values of a society's culture or ideology.[9] On the basis of the irony of the story, Jesus accordingly exhorts his disciples:

> And I say to you, keep on asking, and it will be given to you. Keep on seeking, and you will find; keep on knocking, and it will be opened to you. For everyone who asks receives, and everyone who seeks finds, and to everyone who knocks it will be opened. (11:9–10)

The disciples as petitioners, who address God as Father and keep on asking, seeking, and knocking, can rely on the integrity of God's fatherhood[10] as well as God's response to desperate cries, as presumptuous and ill-mannered as they

---

9. My thanks to Cornelia Cyss-Wittenstein for helping me to resolve the difficulties of this story.

10. The word "fatherhood" is used here only because it corresponds to Jesus' employment of "Father" in his teaching the Lord's Prayer to his disciples. Any reference to God in prayer or discourse must necessarily be metaphorical (see chap. 5).

may be. Jesus establishes that by addressing a rhetorical question to his disciples that presupposes a negative answer: "Which father among you, [when] the son will ask for a fish, will he give him a snake instead of a fish? Or [if] he asks for an egg, will he give him a scorpion?" (Luke 11:11–12). If that holds true for the disciples, that is, if in their parenthood they would not give their children a snake or a scorpion when they had asked for a fish or an egg, the inference that can be drawn for the integrity of God's parenthood is self-evident. And Jesus does not hesitate to draw it:

> If you being wicked know how to give good gifts to your children, how much more will the heavenly Father give the Holy Spirit to those asking him? (11:13)

So we learn something about God in the context of the Lucan version of the Lord's Prayer: God's responsiveness to desperate need and God's reliability toward those who address him as Father. God is not put off by rude manners or outrageous behavior. Moreover, God's integrity as a parent, like the parenthood Jesus attributes to his disciples, is responsible and dependable. It is more predictable because it is nothing less than the integrity of God! Both of these analogies, which attribute to God a character that contradicts the honor/shame way of life of Mediterranean culture, communicate a resolute confidence in God as an iconoclastic but completely reliable parent. Yet as profitable as this accentuation of God's credibility as a Father is, it does little to promote the intelligibility of the prayer's individual petitions. It is necessary, therefore, to review the larger framework of Luke-Acts in order to recover the theological perspective that it conveyed for Christian self-understanding in general and for the praying of the Lord's Prayer in particular.

Both Gospels in which the Lord's Prayer is embedded present a frame of reference for Christian self-understanding that clarifies *who we are before God*. The recovery of such a perspective from the early Christian movement will not only offer correctives to the general understanding of discipleship. It will also enlarge the self-esteem that belongs to Christian identity but is so lamentably lacking. Finally, it will provide a frame of reference from within which the meaning of the Lord's Prayer can be accessed and at the same time prayed more intelligently and responsibly.

Chapter 1

Who Are We Before God?
Christian Self-Understanding
According to the Apostle Paul

The apostle Paul neither cites the Lord's Prayer nor refers to it in his letters. Yet in two different contexts he employs a form of invoking God, an exclamatory form of address that, because of its uniqueness, is almost certainly attributable to the innovation of Jesus.

> Now because you are sons and daughters, God sent forth the Spirit of his Son into our hearts crying, *Abba*, Father.
>
> (Gal. 4:6)

> For you did not receive a spirit of slavery again to fear, but you received a spirit of adoption, by which we cry, *Abba*, Father. (Rom. 8:15)

These references to *Abba*, an Aramaic word meaning "father," occur in contexts in which Paul is reminding his addressees of the extraordinary relationship into which they have been drawn by God's act of adoption and with that act of adoption the attendant gift of God's Spirit. As bearers of God's Spirit, they constitute a household of women and men who have come of age and who therefore are entitled to address their divine Parent as *Abba*. These are features of a new covenant that supersede the privileges of the earlier covenant that the people of Israel had acquired as members of God's first household of faith.[1]

---

1. The word "covenant," as it is used here, refers to a dispensation or a period of time in which a particular kind of relationship exists between two parties who

15

The Status of Israel as Children
in God's Household of Faith

The prophet Jeremiah, in the context of the Babylonian de-
struction of Jerusalem, had enunciated the establishment of a
new covenant between Yahweh and Israel that may be characterized as a paradigm shift, that is, a reconstitution of their
mutual relationship.

> Look, the days are coming, says Yahweh, and I will cut a new
> covenant with the house of Israel and the house of Judah, not
> like the covenant which I cut with their fathers when I took
> hold of their hand to bring them out from the land of Egypt,
> my covenant which they violated, and I was their master, says
> Yahweh. For the covenant, which I will cut with the house
> of Israel after those days, says Yahweh, I will put my Torah
> within them, and on their hearts I will write it; and I will be
> their God, and they will be my people. And no longer will
> they teach each other saying, "Know Yahweh," for they will
> all know me from their least to the greatest, says Yahweh, for
> I will forgive their iniquities, and I will remember their sins
> no longer. (Jer. 31:31–34)

This dramatic shift from one covenantal relationship to
another implies the movement from childhood to adulthood,
from subservience to the law as it was imposed from above
to ethical responsibility authorized and motivated in freedom from within the self of each member of society. Under
the earlier covenant that had been mediated by Moses, Israel was a hierarchically constituted household, and Yahweh
was their benevolent patriarch. According to Genesis 12,
this divine family came into existence when Yahweh called
Abraham and Sarah to leave the fortified city of Ur and the
security it offered, to make themselves vulnerable to the contingencies and terrors of historical existence, and to live by
faith. That was the distinguishing mark of this household.

---

have entered into a binding contract. To differentiate between the old covenant and
the new covenant does not necessarily imply the superiority of the latter over the
former.

It consisted of women, men, and children who were willing to journey with God into an open and unknown future. All those who joined this household would be justified, declared righteous. At the same time, however, they would be subject to the rules and regulations that God, the founder of this family, imposed on them to ensure the practice of justice and peace among them.

Yahweh, as the patriarchal head of this household, was characterized now and then as a father by the prophets and psalmists of Israel.

> Yet, O Yahweh, you are our father, we are the clay, and you are the potter; we are all the work of your hand. (Isa. 64:8)

In this role as Creator, Yahweh sometimes presented himself metaphorically as a woman who gave birth to the members of this divine family.

> Thus says Yahweh who made you, who formed you from the womb and will help you. (Isa. 44:2)

> Listen to me, O house of Jacob, all the remnant of the house of Israel, who have been borne by me from your birth, carried from the womb; even to your old age I am he, and to gray hairs I will carry you. I have made, and I will bear. I will carry and I will save. (Isa. 46:3–4)

Yahweh could be gentle and caring like a mother.

> As one whom his mother comforts, so I will comfort you.
> (Isa. 66:13)

Yahweh could also be forgiving and generous like a father.

> Yahweh is merciful and gracious, slow to anger and abounding in steadfast love. He will not always chide, nor will he keep his anger forever. He does not deal with us according to our sins nor requite us according to our iniquities. For as the heaven is high above the earth, so great is his love toward those who fear him. As far as the east is from the west, so far does he remove our transgressions from us. As a father pities his children, so Yahweh pities those who fear him. For he knows our frame and remembers that we are dust.
> (Ps. 103:8–14)

But the status of the members of this family was always that of minors. They were God's children and therefore subject to their patriarchal parent and the laws that regulated his household. Obedience was required.

> All the commandments which I command you this day you shall be careful to do, that you may live and multiply, and go in and possess the land which Yahweh swore to your ancestors.... Know then in your heart that, as a man disciplines his son, Yahweh your God disciplines you. So you shall keep the commandments of Yahweh your God by walking in his ways and fearing him. (Deut. 8:1, 5–6)

> This day Yahweh your God commands you to do these statutes and ordinances; you shall therefore be careful to do them with all your heart and all your soul. You have declared this day concerning Yahweh that he is your God, and that you will walk in his ways and keep his statutes and his commandments and his ordinances, and obey his voice; and Yahweh has declared this day concerning you that you are a people for his own possession, as he has promised you, and that you are to keep all his commandments, that he will set you high above all nations that he has made, in praise and in fame and in honor, and that you shall be a people holy to Yahweh your God, as he has spoken. (Deut. 26:16–19)

Disobedience was punished, sometimes severely, for Yahweh could also be annoyed, indignant, angry, and even enraged. For the idolatry Israel perpetrated at Mount Sinai after the Exodus, Moses, as Yahweh's spokesman, commanded the Levites:

> "Put your sword on your side, each of you! Go back and forth from gate to gate throughout the camp, and each of you kill your brother, and your friend, and your neighbor." The sons of Levi did as Moses commanded; and about three thousand of the people fell on that day. (Exod. 32:27–28)

Like Moses, the prophets pronounced divine judgment on the household of Israel, above all on its kings and priests who represented God's rule.

At that time, says Yahweh, the bones of the kings of Judah, the bones of its princes, the bones of the priests, the bones of the prophets, and the bones of the inhabitants of Jerusalem shall be brought out of their tombs; and they shall be spread before the sun and the moon and all the host of heaven, which they have loved and served, which they have gone after, and which they have sought and worshiped; they shall not be gathered or buried; they shall be as dung on the surface of the ground. Death shall be preferred to life by the entire remnant that remains of this evil family in all the places where I have driven them.... (Jer. 8:1–3)

The word of Yahweh came to me: "You shall not take a wife, nor shall you have sons or daughters in this place. For thus says Yahweh concerning the sons and daughters who are born in this place, and concerning the mothers who bore them and the fathers who begot them in this land: they shall die of deadly diseases. They shall not be buried; they shall be as dung on the surface of the ground. They shall perish by the sword and by famine, and their dead bodies shall be food for the birds of the air and for the beasts of the earth."

(Jer. 16:1–4)

All of this belongs to the story of Israel, God's first family of faith. It was a covenantal household of men and women who subordinated themselves to the patriarchal rule of God as it was mediated to them through the rules and regulations of the law that were imposed on them by their kings, priests, and prophets.

The Movement from Childhood to Adulthood in God's Household of Faith

The apostle Paul, in his clarification of the Good News of Jesus Christ to the Galatian Christians, designates this first household of faith as a family of children. In their covenantal relationship with God they were heirs, and a divine inheritance awaited them. But they had not yet come of age.

> Now I say, as long as the heir is an infant, he — or she —
> is no better than a slave, [though] he — or she — is lord of
> all things, but is under governors and trustees until the fixed
> time of the father. (Gal. 4:1–2)

Paul then proceeds to draw the application for himself and
the Galatians:

> So with us! When we were children, we were slaves to the
> *stoixeia tou kosmou.* (Gal. 4:3)

The Greek phrase *stoixeia tou kosmou* outside of the
New Testament usually designates the four basic elements of
earth, air, fire, and water, of which the world was believed
to be composed. That is why these three words are usually
translated as "elemental spirits of the world" in Galatians
4:3 and Colossians 2:8. In the New Testament, however,
they have a broader meaning and include all the cultural ar-
tifacts and fetishes that were used by pagans to transcend
historical existence and protect themselves from its contingencies and terrors, namely, myths, philosophy, ceremonies,
rites of passage, rituals of purification, and festivals.[2] In
Galatians 4:9 Paul characterizes these cultural products and
practices as well as the invisible forces that they attempted
to control as "impotent and destitute" because they were
powerless to safeguard human beings from suffering and evil.

The Hebrew Scriptures bear witness that the Israelites and
Jews, instead of living by faith, resorted to similar devices
and stratagems. The purity code of Leviticus[3] established a
system that defined the boundaries of the holy and the pro-
fane, the clean and the unclean, in order to safeguard God's
family from contamination and transgression. Similarly, the
deuteronomistic theology of reciprocity, which is articulated

---

2. For an insightful exposition of the devices and stratagems of archaic peoples
to defend themselves against "the terrors of history," see Mircea Eliade, *Cos-
mos and History: The Myth of the Eternal Return* (New York: Harper & Row
Torchbook, 1959).

3. For example, see the regulations concerning clean and unclean food in
Leviticus 11; the uncleanness of disease in Leviticus 13–15.

in the Book of Deuteronomy, established a process of redemption that was intended to guarantee well-being and security by binding God's family into a relationship of indebtedness and obligation. By obedience to God's commandments Israel could pay back the debt incurred in its deliverance from Egyptian enslavement and the ongoing realization of its potential. These ideological codes that were imposed on the household of Israel may also be identified with the *stoixeia tou kosmou* of Galatians 4:3. Purity and reciprocity served as bonds of obligation to ensure Israel's allegiance to God and consequently the stability and protection they were believed to guarantee for a secure and prosperous future.

The Galatian Christians evidently had reverted to this stage of Israel's childhood by embracing the devices and stratagems of the old covenant to overcome their anxieties and to defend themselves against the absurdities of human existence.[4] As a result, they had become enslaved to the duties and obligations that the Mosaic covenant imposed on God's first family of faith. "You observe days and months and seasons and years," Paul wrote in Galatians 4:10. They were also practicing circumcision. By engaging in excessive ritualism and asceticism, they had tried to make themselves into Jews in order to become Christians. Like the Jews, they were members of God's family, but they had locked themselves into the state of childhood. They had not yet come of age.

No Longer as Children!

According to Paul, however, the work of Jesus Christ, specifically his death and resurrection, marks a decisive point in the course of history.

---

4. Ernest Becker, *The Denial of Death* (New York: The Free Press, 1973), analyzes the character defenses and mechanisms that human beings devise to protect themselves from "the paradox of human existence," that is, being both "a god and a worm," created in God's image and likeness and yet subject to the death of living and the death of dying.

When the fullness of time came, God sent forth his Son, born
from a woman, born under the law, so that he might buy
back [redeem] those under the law, so that we might receive
adoption as sons and daughters. (Gal. 4:4–5)

Originally the Galatians were Gentile pagans, but through
Paul's evangelization they became Christians. As a result of
Jesus' redeeming death, God adopted them and incorporated
them into God's household of faith as daughters and sons,
but not in the stage of childhood.[5] Jesus' death marked the
end of the old moral order of the Mosaic covenant. The
rules and regulations of the law, along with the holiness
code, proved to be ineffective in constituting a society of
justice and peace. Likewise, the deuteronomistic ideology of
reciprocity was impotent in guaranteeing the stability and
security of Israel, as the Book of Job intimated. All they
succeeded in achieving was the disclosure of the human infection of sin; and that, as Paul argued in Galatians 3:19–22,
was the divine objective of the Torah. The law was a mir-
ror that functioned to reveal to human beings their diseased
condition of sin, take them by the hand — like the slave in
antiquity who made certain that a child got to school — and
hand them over to the teacher, Jesus Christ. For "Christ,"
as Paul declared in Romans 10:4, "is the end of the law."
Through the death of Christ the human infection of sin and
the alienation it generates in society are terminated.

For if by the offense of one [Adam] death ruled through the
one [Adam], how much more will those receiving the abun-
dance of grace and the legacy of justice rule in life through
the one Jesus Christ. (Rom. 5:17)

For the death he [Christ] died he died to sin, once for all, but
the life he lives he lives to God. So you also consider yourselves to be dead to sin [the condition] but living to God in
Christ Jesus. (Rom. 6:10–11)

---

5. 1 Corinthians 13:11 might also be quoted in this context: "When I was a
child, I was speaking as a child, I was thinking as a child, I was calculating as a
child. When I became a man [an adult], I did away with childish things."

If the resurrection of Jesus from the dead marks the beginning of a new creation and the establishment of a new humanity, then the death of Jesus signifies the end of the old moral order, the creation that originated with Adam and Eve. At the same time, the condition of sin that permeated the old moral order and dominated all who participated in it is erased. To participate in Jesus' resurrection by means of baptism presupposes the death that immediately preceded it. That is why Paul exhorts, "Consider yourselves dead to sin but living to God in Christ Jesus." To return to the Mosaic covenant and to submit to its rules and regulations, its rites and rituals, is nothing less than a reentry into the stage of childhood. In Galatians 5:1 Paul characterizes it more severely as an act of reenslavement.

Jesus' resurrection establishes the new moral order of the kingdom of God and with it a new humanity. Consequently, as Paul asserts in 2 Corinthians 5:17, "Everyone who is in Christ is a new creation. The old things passed. New things have happened." Among those new things is the fulfillment of Jeremiah's expectation of the enactment of a new covenant: "not of letter but of spirit," according to Paul's differentiation in 2 Corinthians 3:6. The covenant that God established with the first family of faith "came in glory," but it was "chiseled in letters on stone tablets." The new covenant is "written not with ink but with the Spirit of the living God, not on tablets of stone but on tablets of human hearts." Accordingly, the only evidence that Jeremiah's prophecy has been fulfilled and that a new covenant has been enacted is the manifestation of the justice and righteousness God wills in the concrete deeds and activities of human beings. Proceeding from this orientation Paul can identify the Corinthian Christians as "a letter of Christ." As incarnations of God's love, their lives are like a letter or a book that bears witness to the realities of reconciliation and the defeat of death.

The Inheritance of Adulthood:
The Gift of the Holy Spirit

The divine gift that makes the fulfillment of Jeremiah's prophecy possible is the long-awaited inheritance of the Holy Spirit. It is this "Spirit of his Son," as Paul tells the Galatian Christians, that "God sent forth...into our hearts, crying *Abba*, Father." God's act of adoption is accompanied by the gift of the Holy Spirit, the Spirit that resided in Jesus, the Spirit that empowered Jesus to carry out the work that God called him to actualize. To belong to God's household of faith under the new covenant, therefore, means to have come of age, to be an adult of God, and to have received the promised inheritance of God's Holy Spirit. To belong to God's household of faith as adults means to have the new covenant written on the tablets of our hearts by the indwelling of God's Spirit. To be an adult in God's household of faith means to belong to the new humanity of the last Adam, and like Jesus Christ, its founder, to be a life-giving spirit. "The first human being, Adam, became a living soul; the last Adam a life-giving spirit" (1 Cor. 15:45). Christians, as adults of God's household of faith, are distinguished as life-giving spirits. Their identity is their calling. They are ordained to transform the society in which they live, so that they and all their fellow human beings, and eventually the whole creation, will be delivered from the enslavement of living death into the freedom and glory of the new creation (Rom. 8:20–21).

Praying the Lord's Prayer in the Light of
Who We Are Before God

In these letters to the Galatians and the Romans Paul presents a startling perspective of a reconstituted household of faith that serves as the bearer of the kingdom of God and its formidable response-abilities. (The two components of this word are hyphenated in order to avoid the meaning of "duty" or "obligation" and to focus instead on the newly acquired ability to respond through the empowerment of the Holy Spirit.) This actuality of God's rule is the foundation of the church and its mission in the world. Who we are before God derives from this actuality and forms the frame of reference for the liturgy of the church and a meaningful entry into praying the Lord's Prayer. Through our participation in God's household and the horizon of self-understanding that it nurtures the petitions of the Lord's Prayer become transparent and relevant.

The limited sense of Christian self-understanding that is so pervasive in the world prevents Christians from growing out of the stage of childhood into the spiritual maturity of adulthood. The one-sided self-identification of sinner that is embraced in modesty and humility restricts the Good News of Jesus Christ to Good Friday's atoning death of Jesus and the forgiveness that it offers. If what is usually called salvation is reduced to Jesus' death and the reconciliation with God that it constitutes, the result is a lopsided Christian faith. It is also lopsided because it perpetuates a vertical relationship of dependency on God and locks Christians into the stage of childhood.

The Easter event of resurrection defeats death. The Easter event authenticates Jesus as the new Human Being and the beginning of a new humanity. The Easter event establishes the new household of God and confers on all who hold membership in it the privileged status of adult and therefore also partner with God in exercising the authority and power of God's rule.

Moving Beyond Paul into the Gospels of Matthew and Luke

The Lord's Prayer, however, is embedded in the Gospels according to Matthew and Luke. Although Paul, as a representative of the first generation of the Christian movement, stands closer to Jesus than do these Gospels, the interpretation of the Lord's Prayer requires that its petitions are construed in the light of the theological-spiritual perspective of these two Gospels. What frames of reference do Matthew and Luke offer for the elucidation of the Lord's Prayer? What distinguishing realization of identity do they engender that would produce a meaningful entry into the praying of the prayer? And is there a correspondence between the new horizons of self-awareness, which these Gospels convey in and through their individual narrative worlds, and the apostle Paul's accentuation of a new covenant with its implications for a movement from childhood to adulthood in God's household of faith?

Chapter 2

The Frame of Reference from Matthew's Gospel

Matthew's narrative world opens with a genealogical table in which Jesus appears to represent two generations within the history of Israel at the same time. In the third section of this genealogy, "from the Babylonian captivity to the Christ," only thirteen names are listed, although the narrator has stipulated in Matthew 1:17 that, like the previous two sections, fourteen names are to be counted. Within the framework of the number 14, which corresponds to the use of 12 + 2 = 14 in the Messiah Apocalypse of 2 Baruch, Jesus is intimated to be both the thirteenth and fourteenth generations simultaneously. That is, he is linked to the cosmic realities that are associated with these numbers in the numerical scheme of 2 Baruch 69–74.[1] As the representative of the thirteenth generation, Jesus in and through his death on the cross will usher in the divine judgment that terminates the first creation and its sin-infected moral order.[2]

> Now Jesus, crying again with a great voice, sent forth his spirit. And see, the curtain of the sanctuary was split from top to bottom into two, and the earth was shaken and the rocks were split. (Matt. 27:50–51)

As the representative of the fourteenth generation, Jesus will inaugurate a new heaven and a new earth in which a new

---

1. *The Old Testament Pseudepigrapha: Apocalyptic Literature and Testaments*, ed. James H. Charlesworth, 2 vols. (Garden City, N.Y.: Doubleday, 1983), 1:644–46.
2. See H. C. Waetjen, "The Genealogy as the Key to the Gospel according to Matthew," *Journal of Biblical Literature* 95 (June 1976): 205–30.

moral order will be constituted that will eventually include all peoples.

> And the tombs were opened and many bodies of the saints who had fallen asleep were resurrected. And exiting from the tombs after his resurrection, they entered the holy city and were manifested to many. (Matt. 27:52–53)

Jesus as the Son of Man or the New Human Being

This distinctiveness of Jesus' identity, represented by two generations in the construction of the Gospel's opening genealogical table, corresponds to the twofold origin that Matthew ascribes to Jesus. Jesus was generated by God's Spirit. The reality of the virgin birth that is attributed to him implies a new beginning in the history of Israel. Although the Gospel has been introduced by a genealogy that traces his ancestry back to David and Abraham, Jesus, in view of his generation by the Spirit, cannot be affiliated with that family tree and its history. He is a new creation, a new human being, who initially has no connection with the past or the old moral order in which it originated. The old creation, namely, the first creation, according to Genesis 2, was originated by God creating a man from the clay of the earth, making him alive by breathing into his nostrils the breath of life, and subsequently proceeding to fashion a woman from a rib taken from his side. In contrast, the new creation is inaugurated by a woman giving birth to a man who was formed in her womb by God's creative breath, the Holy Spirit. Mary's child, therefore, who like Adam is a creation of God, will be called Emmanuel, "God with us." Accordingly, he will be the bearer of two intimately related christological titles: the Son of Man and the Son of God.

Jesus' identity as the Son of God depends on his generation by the Holy Spirit and his Adamlike origin as a new human being within the womb of Mary, the Virgin. To say it in another way, he is the Son of God because he is the Son of Man. His identity as the Son of Man, however, does not refer only to his human nature, as is all too frequently assumed. For "the Son of Man" is a designation that is derived from the millennialism of Jewish apocalypticism, specifically the figure of "one like a human being" of Daniel 7:13. By identifying Jesus with this divine being whose coming was anticipated in the imminent future, the earliest Christians stipulated him to be an Adamlike personage who came out of the future in order to constitute a new humanity. To entitle Jesus as the Son of Man is to confer on him the distinction of being the first final human being and attendantly the progenitor of a new human race. Consequently, "the new Human Being" is a more appropriate appellation in place of the traditional phrase "the Son of Man," because it conveys the eschatological reality of his identity and is linguistically inclusive.

At the same time this reality of the new Human Being, in view of its derivation from the figure of "one like a human being" (Dan. 7:13), must also be apprehended as a corporate reality. The Son of Man or the new Human Being is a community as well as an individual. Daniel 7:22 and 27 interpret the figure of "one like a human being" as "the saints of the Most High."

> until the Ancient of Days came, and judgment was given for the saints of the Most High, and the time came when the saints received the kingdom. (Dan. 7:22)

> And the kingship and the dominion and the greatness of the kingdoms under the whole heaven shall be given to the people of the saints of the Most High. Their kingdom shall be an everlasting kingdom, and all dominions shall serve and obey them. (Dan. 7:27)

The Son of Man or the new Human Being, therefore, is like Uncle Sam in the United States. He is representative of the

reality of "the One and the Many."[3] Those who participate in this community of the One and the Many share a
horizontal status and relationship in which each member of
the community is both an individual expression of the new
Human Being (like Jesus) as well as a representative of the
corporate new humanity (like Jesus). No purity code is oper-
ative which would establish a pollution system and divide the
world into the dualistic realms of the clean and the unclean.
Jesus, the new Human Being, who even more than Adam is
God's offspring, moves away from a dichotomized world of
binary oppositions into a universal actualization of the One
and the Many.

Jesus as the Messiah, the Son of David

The Old Testament trajectory of prophetic eschatology and
its Son of David christology are united with this millennial
perspective of Jesus as the new Human Being, the Son of
God. In Matthew's narrative world it is expressed by Joseph's
adoption of Jesus, an act that incorporates him into Joseph's
family tree and accordingly into the dynasty of David, the
ancestry of Abraham and Sarah, and the history of Israel.
By being obedient to the angelic command, taking Mary as
his wife, and naming Jesus (1:24–25), Joseph declares himself to be his father. Consequently Jesus becomes the Son of
David, the Messiah, or, as the Magi call him, "the king of
the Jews." In terms of this identity he, like David and the
kings of the Davidic dynasty, is acknowledged to be God's
son, as Psalm 2:7 witnesses. Like David, and in fulfillment of
Micah 5:2, Jesus is born in Bethlehem. Ironically, however,
he cannot fulfill his identity as the Son of David in the land of
Israel, the designation of the province of Judea in Matthew
2:20–21, because of the threat that Herod the Great's son,

3. See Kenelm Burridge, *New Heaven-New Earth: A Study of Millenarian
Activities* (New York: Schocken, 1969), 107–12, 145–49.

Archelaus, poses. Subsequently the incarceration of his fore-runner, John the Baptizer, also endangers his life and forces him to withdraw into Galilee. Nevertheless, Galilee, as the quotation of Matthew 4:15 indicates, is the territory of Ze-bulon and Naphtali, tribal lands of Old Testament Israel, and therefore Jesus can discharge his messiahship in this region.

Inaugurating the Kingdom or the Rule of God

The ministry that Jesus conducts throughout Matthew's nar-rative world is primarily ethnocentric or nationalistic in character, but it ushers in the new moral order of God's rule that Daniel had anticipated. Although Jesus is first and fore-most the new Human Being, generated by the Holy Spirit, his identity as the Davidic ruler who comes from Bethlehem and who "will shepherd God's people Israel" determines the character of his ministry (2:6). His mission, therefore, is lim-ited to Israel, as he himself insists in his encounter with the Canaanite woman: "I was not sent except to the lost sheep of the house of Israel" (15:24). His messianic activity will in-volve him in delivering his fellow Jews from the oppression of the old moral order and the tyranny of its system of ritual cleansing. He is conspicuously compassionate toward "the crowds," "for they were harassed and driven like sheep not having a shepherd" (9:36). He does not "separate the wheat from the chaff," as John the Baptizer had predicted. His min-istry will not be determined by any purity code. When John, disturbed by this unexpected character of Jesus' messiahship, sends his disciples to inquire whether he is indeed the Christ, Jesus replies, "Go [and] report to John the things you hear and see: the blind gain sight and the lame walk, lepers are cleansed and the deaf hear, and the dead are raised and the poor are evangelized. And privileged with divine favor is the one who is not scandalized by me" (Matt. 11:4–6). While the Son of David messiahship of Jesus dominates Matthew's

presentation of Jesus' career, it is modified and reoriented by
the universalistic as well as the corporate character of his
identity as the new Human Being. Accordingly, the objective
of his ministry is constituting "the kingdom of God," not
"the kingdom of David" (12:28). Consequently, in spite of
his ethnocentric attitude, Jesus occasionally confers the benefits of his messianic activity on outsiders. In these instances
his identity as the new Human Being and its universalistic
orientation supersede his nationalistic disposition. So, for example, when he is moved and overcome by the extraordinary
faith of a Roman centurion, he heals the centurion's servant
and concomitantly enunciates the eventual outcome of his
ministry:

> I tell you that many will come from east and west and will
> recline at table with Abraham and Isaac and Jacob in the
> kingship of the heavens. But the sons [and daughters] of the
> kingship will be thrown into outer darkness, and there will
> be weeping and gnashing of teeth. (8:11–12)

Jesus' encounter with the Canaanite woman in 15:21–
28 culminates in the exorcism of her daughter, in spite his
initial refusal to respond to her plea. She will not be put
off, not even by his denigrating reference to "her kind" as
"house dogs." When she fails to gain a hearing, after having approached him as "Lord, Son of David," she omits the
title that conveys his ethnocentric messiahship, and addressing him simply as "Lord," she insists that "the house dogs
eat the crumbs [as they] fall from the table of their lords"
(15:27). Although she is an outsider and a representative
of the subjugated Canaanites, she unhesitatingly acknowledges her rightful access to the benefits of his messiahship.
The reader may well conclude that through this encounter
Jesus' ethnocentric messiahship is being stretched to include
non-Jews.

Jesus acknowledges Simon Peter's confessional identification, "You are the Christ, the Son of the living God," by
favoring him with the title of Petros (Rock), or more pre-

cisely, since the word is an adjective, Rocky (Matt. 16:18). Yet at the outset of his interrogation of the disciples about his identity, he revealed his preference for the appellation that is based on his generation by the Holy Spirit: "Who do human beings say that the new Human Being is?" The transfiguration, which shortly follows Jesus' inquiry about his identification among the people and his disciples, discloses the divinity of his identity as the new Human Being: "This is my beloved Son in whom I began to take pleasure." And to ensure that it is his deification as the new Human Being, not as the Messiah, that the transfiguration has unveiled, Jesus charges his disciples to tell no one of the vision "until the new Human Being was raised from the dead" (17:9).

Jesus as the Messiah and the New Human Being

Matthew's narration of the triumphal entry into Jerusalem is unique among those of the Evangelists, for it features the extraordinary act of Jesus riding on two donkeys at the same time. Two disciples are commanded to fetch two animals, a donkey *(onos)* and a colt *(pôlos)*. Accordingly, "they led the donkey and the colt, and they placed clothing on them, and he sat over them" (21:7). The two beasts, particularly as they are associated with Zechariah 9:9, are representative of Jesus' paradoxical identities.[4] The donkey *(onos)* is the coronation animal on which he ironically rides to his enthronement on the cross as the king of the Jews. The "colt, son of an animal under yoke" *(pôlon huion hypozygiou)*, is the beast of burden he rides as the new Human Being, who, according to 8:17, "took our sicknesses and carried our dis-

---

4. The donkey and the colt are linked to the fulfillment of Zechariah 9:9, but their employment in Matthew's version of the triumphal entry is not a matter of misunderstanding the poetic parallelism of Zechariah. The Evangelist identifies the colt as "the offspring of an animal under yoke," a commercial beast of burden.

eases." Jesus' identity as the new Human Being is linked to servanthood, particularly as it is characterized by Isaiah 53. These two donkeys, analogous to the two hats people claim to wear to express dual roles or offices they occupy, signify the two identities Jesus bears as he rides into Jerusalem at this climactic moment in his career. The narrator observes that the city quaked *(eseisthê)* at his entry (21:10). Jesus' death terminates both of these identities and the offices or roles that are connected to them. His crucifixion as the Messiah concludes the old covenant and with it the privileged identity of Israel as the elect people of God. The rending of the temple veil, accordingly, testifies to the departure of the divine presence from its Jerusalem residence. Jesus' crucifixion as the new Human Being plunges the creation into primordial chaos and brings the old moral order to an end.

> Now Jesus again crying with a great voice sent forth his spirit. And see, the veil of the sanctuary was split from top to bottom into two, and the earth was shaken *(eseisthê)* and the rocks were split. (27:50–51)

The first sign of a new creation follows this cataclysmic event:

> The tombs were opened and many bodies of the saints [who] had been asleep were resurrected. (27:52)

The Resurrection and the New Humanity

With the resurrection of the Old Testament saints, the long-awaited reconstitution of all things has begun. The new moral order that they had anticipated has dawned, and they are its first participants. Jesus, of course, was the first to have been raised from the dead, so it is natural for the narrator to specify the priority of his resurrection. Yet in one respect the saints precede him, although they do not emerge from their tombs until after his resurrection. Causally linked to

Jesus' death, their awakening is the result of his final exhalation (27:50).[5] His is the breath, as Emmanuel, "God with us," that breathes into these dead ones and makes them alive again. Here is an echo of Ezekiel 37:9–12. For after being awakened from the sleep of death, they must await his own exit from the grave so that he can lead them, in accordance with Ezekiel 37:12: "I am opening your tombs, and I will lead you up from your tombs, and I will lead you into the land of Israel."

An earthquake also signals the resurrection of Jesus and with it the actualization of the new creation (28:2). Jesus himself is the pioneer; and his disciples, the community of the new Human Being that he constitutes, are co-enthroned with him and deputized to universalize the actualized reality of God's rule. After presenting himself to the two women, his mother Mary and Mary Magdalene, who will serve as the witnesses of the reality of his resurrection, he subsequently appears to eleven of the twelve representatives of the new Israel he had chosen before his death. He addresses them in terms of his identity as the new Human Being and the fulfillment of Daniel 7:13–14 that his resurrection has effected: "All authority in heaven and on earth was given to me" (Matt. 28:18). As his representatives they are commissioned to "make disciples of all the nations," baptizing them into the new creation and transmitting to them the teaching they have received from him (28:19–20).

Eleven ascended into the mountain; twelve descend.[6] This is not explicitly stated by the narrator, but it is implied by the final verse of the Gospel, 28:20. Jesus does not remain behind on the mountain, nor does he ascend into heaven. He joins himself to the company of the Eleven: "See, *I* with you *am* even to the consummation of the age." As the twelfth, therefore, he reconstitutes Israel and imparts to its repre-

---

5. This is a deduction based on the reading of the Greek text, translated literally, "And Jesus, crying again with a loud voice, sent forth the Spirit."
6. Read Matthew 28:16 and 28:20 in relation to each other.

sentatives both his identity and his empowerment as the new Human Being. They are what he is, and what he has done they will do because he will be with them. Accordingly, the new Human Being is no longer only an individual but also a community or a communion; and this communion of the new Human Being is embraced by his divine "I am." For according to the word order of the Greek text of this final declaration, the prepositional phrase "with you" is enclosed by the "I am": "See, I with you am even to the consummation of the age." The new Human Being whom they, according to 1:23, "will call 'Emmanuel,' that is, God with us," makes a commitment to accompany them to the consummation of history.

The New Moral Order of God's Rule and the Self-Understanding It Engenders

Membership in this reconstituted Israel, this community of the new Human Being, requires the appropriation of the twofold origin that is attributed to Jesus. Like him, his disciples wear two hats. On the one hand, they are new human beings, generated by the Holy Spirit, who have been entrusted with the sovereignty of the kingdom in order to fulfill the Great Commission Jesus issued to them on the mountain in Galilee. On the other hand, they are still participants in the old moral order, subject to the infection of sin that was socialized into them by their parents and the society into which they were born. Nevertheless, like Jesus, they are to regard themselves as royalty, but royalty dedicated to the work of justice and peace in society.

This double bind of Christian identity may express itself in the lives of God's daughters and sons in the same parallel trajectories that are manifested in Matthew's account of Jesus' ministry. To participate in the new humanity and exercise the sovereignty of God's rule presupposes an inclusive, universalistic outlook that is accompanied by a nomadic style of life.

> The foxes have dens and the birds of the sky will nest, but the new Human Being [and by extension, the new humanity] has nowhere to lay his head. (8:20)

At the same time, their self-understanding as sinners involves them in an identification with their fellow human beings who are still imprisoned in the old moral order. In this mode of consciousness they are ethnically oriented, like Jesus. They feed the hungry, clothe the naked, show hospitality to strangers, care for the sick, and visit those in prison, but first of all among the people of their own nationality, or their own race, or their own denominational membership. The invisible letter they wear, S, representing both saint and sinner, is the symbol of their calling.

The context for this self-understanding is the actuality of God's rule as it continues to permeate the old moral order. The church, or in Matthew's narrative world, the new Israel as the household of God, participates in both worlds. Within this frame of reference the church conducts its worship of God, nourishes the double bind of Christian identity, and accordingly promotes the responsible praying of the Lord's Prayer.

Chapter 3

The Frame of Reference
from Luke-Acts

In the two-volume literary composition of Luke-Acts the reader enters a narrative world different from that of Matthew. The genealogy of Jesus, with which Matthew introduced his Gospel, is presented in Luke's Gospel immediately after Jesus' baptism. Moreover, Luke begins with Jesus himself, who is qualified as "being a son, as it was thought, of Joseph" (3:23), in order to safeguard his distinctive origin in the light of his virgin birth. Moving backwards, the genealogy climaxes with "Adam, God's son" (3:38), evidently in order to reinforce the reality of the virgin birth, that Jesus, in view of his generation by the Holy Spirit, is both a type and an antitype of the first Adam and like him is to be identified simultaneously as God's Son and as the inaugurator of a new humanity.

John the Baptizer, whose circumstances of birth are elaborated, signifies the end of the old moral order. "The Law and the Prophets were until John," as Jesus enunciates in 16:16. His parents, Zechariah and Elizabeth, who like Abraham and Sarah are childless but nevertheless empowered to generate a son, bring the history of Israel full circle. The end is like the beginning. But the end will be marked by an apocalyptic event, namely, God's judgment on the old moral order. John, as the angel Gabriel foretells Zechariah at the temple altar of incense, will be God's predecessor, "going before him [the Lord God] in the spirit and power of Elijah" (1:17). According to Zechariah's Benedictus, John will be called "the prophet of the Most High," and as such his mission will be to impart the millennial knowledge of the coming salvation to God's people, Israel.

The Virgin Birth of Jesus in Luke's Gospel

The apocalyptic event of God's salvation is the inauguration of the kingdom of God. It will be enacted by Jesus, God's offspring and, attendantly, according to the virgin birth, the new Adam. As in Matthew's narrative world, the virgin birth establishes discontinuity with the history of Israel, but in Luke's Gospel that discontinuity is more universally oriented and, according to the genealogy of 3:23–38, comprehends the entire history of humankind, moving beyond Abraham and Sarah back to Adam and Eve.

The beginning of this new humanity stands in contrast to that of the old. Instead of the woman being fashioned from a rib of a man (Gen. 2:21), a man is birthed by a woman in whom this new human being has been generated by the power of the Most High. The woman, Mary, in her acceptance of the divine role she is called to fulfill, is representative of virgin Israel who in her self-acknowledgment as "a slave woman of the Lord" collaborates with God for the work of world reconstruction. The Magnificat, which Mary composes in 1:46–55, expresses the social revolution that her divinely originating pregnancy has already inaugurated.

The initial identification of this male that Mary is given by the angel Gabriel at the annunciation is Son of the Most High, a designation that bears an apocalyptic stamp by its use of the epithet "Most High" that is commonly ascribed to God in Jewish apocalypticism.[1] As God's own offspring and simultaneously a new Adam, Jesus will bear the title "the Son of Man" in the narrative world of Luke-Acts. As such

---

1. See Daniel 2:25, 32, 34; 5:18, 21; 7:18, 22, 25, 27.

he will be co-bearer of the divine appellation "Lord" and
serve as God's surrogate to bring about the new moral order
of God's rule.[2] He will heal the sick, cleanse lepers, feed the
hungry, deliver individuals from the oppression of the purity
code, raise the dead, exorcise demons, and manifest his divine sovereignty over the realm of chaos by stilling the storm.
And when he is challenged by the guardians of the old moral
order, he will identify his activities with the actualization of
God's rule: "If by the finger of God I cast out demons, the
rule of God has overtaken you" (11:20).

In addition to this distinguishing certification of Jesus as
the Son of the Most High and the Son of Man who inaugurates the millennial activity of world reconstruction, Luke,
like the Evangelist Matthew, has also adopted the christology
of the messianic Son of David. At the annunciation Mary
is promised that this child of divine origin, which she will
bear, will inherit "the throne of his father David, and he will
rule over the house of Jacob forever, and of his rule there
will be no end" (1:32–33). In time the irony of this pledge
will become apparent to the reader. More immediately, however, the basis of Jesus' relationship to David is and remains
an enigma. Jesus, like David, is born in Bethlehem; and like
Solomon, the son of David, he is swathed by his mother to
signify his royalty.[3] The angelic announcement to the shep-
herds identifies this newborn savior by juxtaposing the two
epithets by which he will be called ("Christ Lord") and at
the same time by distinguishing him as "being swathed" as a
mark of identification (2:11–12).

Jesus is the Christ, but "Christ," as a designation of Jesus,
tends to stand alone except in two instances where it is
linked to "Lord" and "God." In 2:26 the narrator informs
us that Simeon had been promised he would not die until
he saw "the Christ of [the] Lord." He will be the bearer

---

2. Luke 2:11; 5:8; 6:5; 7:6, 13, 19; 9:54; 10:1; 11:1; 12:41–42; 13:15, 23;
17:6, 37; 18:6, 41; 19:8, 31, 34; 22:33, 38; 24:34.

3. See Wisdom of Solomon 7:4 and Longus, *Daphnis and Chloe* 1,2.

of God's salvation, first as "a light for a revelation of the nations" and then also as the glory of God's people, Israel. Here is another instance in the narrative world of Luke-Acts in which the universality of Jesus' mission has precedence over his immediate ethnically oriented ministry. In contrast to Matthew's prioritization of Jesus as the messianic Son of David "who was sent to the lost sheep of the house of Israel," Luke's Gospel has subordinated Jesus' Davidic messiahship to the identity he bears as the result of the virgin birth. Although the demons and unclean spirits know that he is "the Christ" (4:41) and Simon Peter confesses him to be "the Christ of God" (9:20), Jesus' messiahship is fundamentally determined by the priority of Jewish millenarism and the christological titles derived from it. Jesus is the anointed Son of the Most High and, as the new Adam, the Son of Man, he is the founder of a new and universal humanity.

At his arrival in Jerusalem, riding on a donkey, Jesus is welcomed as "the king who comes in the name of the Lord." Accordingly, it would appear that the promise of the angel Gabriel to Mary will finally be fulfilled: "The Lord God will give to him the throne of his father David, and he will rule over the house of Israel forever." Jesus himself, however, will pose the christological riddle by challenging the ruling elite with the puzzle of Psalm 110:1.

> How do they say [that] the Christ is the Son of David? For David himself says in the Book of Psalms: "The Lord said to my Lord, 'Keep on sitting at my right hand until I place your enemies under your feet.'" David therefore calls him Lord, and how is he his son?

Evidently David's Lord is not his son! Jesus, therefore, while he is rightly acknowledged as the Christ or the Christ of God, is fundamentally misinterpreted and misrepresented as the Son of David. On the basis of his virgin birth he is essentially a new human being who is also the Son of the Most High and therefore discontinuous with history and its infected moral order.

Luke's Use of the Exodus Theme
to Interpret Jesus' Work

As his dialogue with Moses and Elijah on the Mount of Transfiguration reveals, Jesus is engaged in initiating a new exodus (9:31), and his march to Jerusalem, which commences in 9:51, is a journey into the heart of darkness — analogous to all that Egypt symbolized in the Old Testament story of the Exodus — in which ironically a new and greater deliverance will be enacted. The Exodus of old is commemorated with the first cup of wine that Jesus offers his apostles in 22:17, and the new and forthcoming exodus, which inaugurates "the new covenant," is celebrated with the second cup (22:20). In the same context Jesus transfers the rule of God, which he has established, to his followers:

> You are the ones who have continued with me in my testings; and I assign to you, even as my Father assigned to me, a kingdom. (22:28–29; see Luke 12:32)

The Acts of the Apostles will narrate the story of their empowerment and their subsequent extension of this new moral order from Jerusalem and Judea into Samaria and the ends of the earth (Acts 1:8).

The salvation event of the new exodus begins, like the old Exodus, with death, the death of Jesus. With profound irony the words that Gabriel spoke to Mary at the annunciation are fulfilled. Jesus' elevation on the cross is his enthronement as the king of the Jews. This is the manner in which he will "sit in the throne of his father David." Moreover, as a result of this ironic enthronement in crucifixion, he is more than David's son. He is David's Lord! For his crucifixion originates a new exodus. But in contrast to the old Exodus, the new exodus is constituted as a cosmic event: "darkness came upon the whole earth until the ninth hour, as the sun failed" (23:44–45). A mythical eclipse — mythical because an eclipse at the time of a full moon is impossible — signals judgment and the end of the old moral order. Like the waters of the Red Sea that "were divided" at the time of the old Exodus, the curtain of the sanctuary is "divided in the middle," and the new exodus is inaugurated as God vacates the temple in fulfillment of Jesus' words in 13:35, "See, your house is left to you."[4]

The new exodus continues to unfold on Easter morning as the women encounter "two men in dazzling garments" in the tomb of Jesus (24:3). They must be Moses and Elijah, the representatives of the Law and the Prophets, who were seen on the Mount of Transfiguration "in glory" and who conversed with Jesus about the "exodus he was going to fulfill in Jerusalem" (9:31). They have reappeared to bear witness to the reality of fulfillment.

The Exodus from Jerusalem into the Mediterranean World in the Acts of the Apostles

But the salvation event of the new exodus must be consummated. Accordingly the exodus motif is extended into volume 2, the Acts of the Apostles. After his resurrection Jesus remains with his disciples for forty days and, like Moses at the end of the forty-year trek through the wilderness, ascends a mountain and is transported by a cloud into heaven. The journey of his exodus, which began in Luke 9:51, has been completed; and at the same time the apocalyptic vision of Daniel 7:13–14 has been realized. Jesus, by being taken up into heaven and receiving "dominion, glory, and kingship," has been co-enthroned with the Ancient of Days. In the consummation of this long exodus journey he has been confirmed as David's Lord. Once more Moses and

---

4. Stephen, one of the seven deacons, who is the first among the earliest Christians to acknowledge that God does not dwell in houses made with human hands. See Acts 7:48.

Elijah, who according to tradition were distinguished by their ascension into heaven, appear to testify to this climactic reality of apocalyptic fulfillment (Acts 1:10).

Moreover, Jesus' exodus journey as the new Human Being, the Son of God, is simultaneously a corporate eschatological reality in which the community of Jesus' disciples participates. At Pentecost, fifty days after the new exodus, a new people of God, a new Israel, emerge after the disciple Matthias has been divinely chosen by lot to fill the vacancy that the apostasy of Judas has left in the patriarchal circle of the Twelve (Acts 1:23–26). All who are gathered together in the upper room of Jerusalem as the disciples of the enthroned Son of Man experience the fulfillment of John the Baptizer's promise: "He will baptize you with the Holy Spirit and with fire" (Luke 3:16). They are the first members of the new household God establishes on the basis of the fulfillment of the new exodus. They receive both the gift of God's Spirit and the tongue of fire as the mark of their new identity as God's beloved sons and daughters. As bearers of the divine flame, they are confirmed in their new status as the divinely crowned representatives of "God's rule, the legacy that Jesus bequeathed to them at the celebration of the Passover and its institution of the Lord's supper."[5] As bearers of the Holy Spirit they are empowered to exercise that legacy of God's rule and to fulfill the commission Jesus gave them in Acts 1:8 before his ascension: "to be his witnesses in Jerusalem and in all Judea and Samaria and to the ends of the earth."

The first day of their apostolic witness manifests the realities of the new moral order: the reversal of the confusion of languages and the cancellation of the old covenant. Simon Peter's Pentecost address to an audience of Jews from many different parts of the Greco-Roman world is understood by all who are present who "hear in [their] own language" the

---

5. See Richard Oster, "Numismatic Windows into the Social World of Early Christianity: A Methodological Inquiry," *Journal of Biblical Literature* 101 (June 1982): 212–14.

good news he is proclaiming to them (Acts 2:8). The outcome is that "those who received his word were baptized, and there were added that day about three thousand souls" (Acts 2:41). Pentecost stands in stark contrast to the idolatry Israel perpetrated at Sinai fifty days after the old Exodus. Moses not only smashed the tablets of the covenant; he also sent the Levites through the camp of Israel and they put to death "about three thousand men" (Exod. 32:26–28). The covenant Jesus has enacted is a covenant of life. It is also a covenant of reconciliation and reunion. It builds a new family that is universally inclusive and horizontally constituted in which each member, as a bearer of God's Spirit, has come of age and attained the status of an adult of God. Luke offers a glimpse of these earliest adult women and men of God's new household in Acts 2:44–47:

> Now all who believed were together; they had all things in common; and they sold their possessions and goods and distributed them to all, as any had need. And day by day, attending the temple together and breaking bread in their homes, they partook of food with gladness and simplicity of heart, praising God and having favor with all the people. And the Lord was adding to them day by day those who were being saved.

The Lucan Frame of Reference

According to Luke, and in agreement with Matthew's Gospel, the new moral order of God's rule is the frame of reference within which Jesus conducted his ministry. In the Acts of the Apostles it is also the frame of reference within which Peter and Paul evangelized Jews, Greeks, and Romans. Although these Gospels were not addressed to human beings who are living today, their witness to the present reality of God's rule as the foundation of the church and its self-understanding confronts and challenges the church as it moves into a new millennium as well as a new century.

Chapter 4

A First-Century Frame of Reference for Interpreting the Lord's Prayer Today

The Evangelists Matthew and Luke, through their independently constructed narrative worlds, present the establishment of the new moral order of God's rule and within it, as its representative, the household of God's adult sons and daughters. This household is both discontinuous and continuous with the household of the old covenant. It is discontinuous because it involves the inauguration of a new creation and with it a new humanity. It is continuous because it is grounded in the faith of Israel and the fulfillment of the divine promises communicated to Israel by its own prophets. This household of God, which Jesus reconstitutes, is both universal and inclusive. It extends beyond the boundaries of ethnicity and nationhood as well as the confines of any and every purity code. Jesus, as influenced as he may have been in his personhood and activity by his Jewish ethnicity, is irrevocably determined by his virgin birth as the new Human Being. As a result of his work, all his followers down through the centuries constitute a divine family, and in their horizontal relationship to him and to God they are bearers of the same human-divine self-understanding that the Gospels according to Matthew and Luke attribute to him. In their consciousness, therefore, they are to embrace their primary identity as new human beings and participants in God's new moral order of justice and equality. At the same time, they are constrained to embrace their identity as sinners and with it their solidarity with their fellow human beings who continue to be locked into the old moral order and suffer under the realities of injustice, oppression, and dispossession.

Christian consciousness is a consciousness of ambiguity: being mature yet immature, complete yet incomplete, perfect yet imperfect. It is a self-understanding of being both saint and sinner. Saints who, as members of God's reconstituted family, are collaborating with God in the transformation of the world. Sinners whom God has destined to participate in that divine royalty that Jesus manifested in his transfiguration. As Jesus said at the conclusion of his interpretation of the parable of the wheat and the darnels:

> Then the just will shine as the sun in the kingdom of their Father. (Matt. 13:43)

The Lord's Prayer, therefore, is the prayer of those who are growing into the full stature of Jesus Christ through the indwelling activity of God's Spirit and consequently realizing the potentiality of their heritage as God's beloved daughters and sons. Because of their participation in God's rule, they have been elevated to royalty, and through their co-enthronement with their Pioneer, Jesus Christ, "the firstborn of many brothers and sisters," they are destined to share with him the rule of the world. Embracing their royal identity, they pray the Lord's Prayer, voicing their support of the activities God has initiated, and instinctively they engage in those activities in order to fulfill their call and complete God's work of world transformation.

However, in their self-understanding as adult members of God's household, they do not live according to any purity code. No such system determines their relationship to their fellow human beings. They do not divide the world and all that is in it into the realms of the clean and the unclean. While they are adults, they are also like children. For like children, who have not yet differentiated the realities of the

world and its people into the opposed categories of the good
and the bad, they retain a childlike openness and vulnerability to the world in which they live. Evil is real and is not to
be minimized or dismissed. But no one and nothing are pre-
judged to be evil or good prior to experience. Consequently,
those who participate with Jesus in the new humanity he established are liable to suffer many things because they are
not protected by any purity code, dualistic worldview, or
system of binary oppositions.

From within this more or less common perspective that
has been derived from the letters of Paul and the Gospels
according to Matthew and Luke the content of the Lord's
Prayer will be illuminated. As old as this frame of reference
is, it can still enrich Christian self-understanding, promote
meaningful prayer, and make the contemporary praying of
the Lord's Prayer intelligent and responsible.

Chapter 5

The Invocation and the First Petition

"Father, your name be held in awe."

God has been invoked with many different forms of address in the Judeo-Christian tradition. Before the Sinai revelation God was identified with Israel's eponymous patriarchs: "the God of Abraham," "the God of Isaac," "the God of Jacob." "Yahweh" was the name God disclosed to Moses for authentication to the enslaved Hebrews in Egypt. But eventually "Adonai," a Jewish circumlocution meaning "my Lord," was substituted in order to preserve the sanctity of the divinely revealed name. As a result, the appellation "Yahweh" was read as "Adonai" by those who produced the Septuagint, the Greek translation of the Hebrew Scriptures, and therefore rendered as "Kyrie," meaning "Lord." Subsequently "Lord," a masculine title that denotes power and sovereignty, a title that the landed gentry reserved for itself, has become one of the most widely used invocations of God in both Jewish and Christian prayers. More recently forms of address like "Creator," "Redeemer," "Savior," and "Sustainer" have become more popular in an effort to avoid attributing gender to God. These epithets derive from verbs that acknowledge particular activities attributable to God. As for the designation "God," it is not a name but rather a common noun that identifies a class of objects, like the words "tree," "flower," and "animal."

The Invocation: Father

"Father," as an invocation of God, is more distinctive. Although it also was an ancient form of addressing the deity, its use appears to have been extremely limited. In the Babylonian creation myth, the *Enuma Elish*, the gods refer to their paternal parents and grandparents as father and on occasion even address them as such. But the gods themselves are never invoked as father or mother by their human petitioners.

The Hebrew Scriptures, however, mark a significant turning point. God is not only compared with an earthly father, as in Psalm 103:13.

> As a father has compassion for his children, so Yahweh has compassion for those fearing him.

God is also designated father, as in Psalm 89:26.

> He will cry to me, "You are my Father, my God, and the Rock of my salvation."

God is named or addressed as father fifteen times in the Hebrew Scriptures.[1] God as a father is also implied in all those instances in which Israel or Israel's king is called God's son.

> When Israel was a child, I loved him, and out of Egypt I called my son. (Hos. 11:1)

> I will speak of the decree of Yahweh: he said to me, "You are my son! Today I have begotten you." (Ps. 2:7)

But in these and other such instances God's fatherhood intimates generative power. God is the Creator, and, like a mother, God gives birth to Israel and to Israel's king. This distinguishing kinship is accentuated by the prophets in order to remind the people of Israel and Judah of their divine origin and of the intimacy of their relationship to their divine parent which that origin presupposes.

---

1. Deuteronomy 32:6; Jeremiah 3:4, 19; 31:9; 2 Samuel 7:14 paralleled by 1 Chronicles 17:13; 22:10; 28:6; Isaiah 63:16; 64:8; Malachi 1:6; 2:10; Psalm 68:5, 89:26.

I thought how I would set you among my children and give you a pleasant land, the most beautiful heritage of all the nations. And I thought you would call me, "my Father," and would not turn from following me. (Jer. 3:19)

With weeping they will come, and with consolations I will lead them back. I will make them walk by brooks of water, in a straight path in which they will not stumble. For I am a father to Israel, and Ephraim is my firstborn. (Jer. 31:9)

For you are our father, though Abraham does not know us, and Israel does not acknowledge us. You, O Yahweh, are our father, our Redeemer from of old is your name. (Isa. 63:16)

Yahweh is the lord or master of this divinely constituted family. In all these acknowledgments of God as father, the prevailing structure of patriarchy is presupposed. That is, Yahweh's fatherhood is regarded to be analogous to the male head of an Israelite or a Jewish household. Having "reared and brought up" these sons and daughters, Yahweh regards "himself" to be their parent and indeed their owner.[2]

The ox knows its owner, and the ass its master's crib; but Israel does not know, my people does not understand.

(Isa. 1:3)

As the father of Israel, who gave birth to both the nation and its king, Yahweh does not hesitate to remind the members of his family of his absolute sovereignty. In the so-called allegory of the potter Jeremiah enunciates this sense of God's supremacy over Israel:

O house of Israel, can I not do with you as the potter has done? See, like the clay in the potter's hand, so are you in my hand, O house of Israel. (Jer. 18:6)

Second Isaiah articulates a vision that accentuates Yahweh's transcendence and power.

Have you not heard? Have you not known? Have you not understood from the foundations of the earth? It is he who sits above the circle of the earth, and its inhabitants are like

---

2. The implication of Isaiah 1:3.

grasshoppers; who stretches out the heavens like a curtain
and spreads them like a tent to dwell in; who brings princes
to nothing and makes the rulers of the earth as nothing.
(Isa. 40:21–23)

To whom then will you compare me, or who is my equal?
Lift up your eyes on high and see: who created these? He
who brings out their host and numbers them, calling them all
by name; because he is great in strength, mighty in power,
not one is missing. (Isa. 40: 25–26)

Israel's status and stature within God's household are determined by a covenant of reciprocity. Obedience is required
and will be rewarded by God's generosity.[3] Defiance and
rebellion, however, will be severely penalized. Ezekiel, as
Yahweh's spokesman, can portray Israel as an abandoned
girl who is not only adopted into God's household and cared
for but also is eventually joined to "him" in marriage and
elevated to world renowned queenship (16:1–14). When,
however, she lapses into religious infidelity through foreign
alliances, Yahweh threatens divorce and with it the loss of
her fortunes. By entering into a covenant of reciprocity, the
people of Israel have committed themselves to a relationship
of obligation. In exchange for their deliverance from Egyptian enslavement they pledge themselves to membership in
God's household. Accordingly, they submit to the statutes
and ordinances that will determine their life and relationships within this household; and in return they will be amply
recompensed by God's loyalty. The binding mutuality that
conditions the life of this divine family is singularly expressed
by the Book of Deuteronomy.

And if you will obey my commandments which I command
you this day, to love Yahweh your God and to serve him with
all your heart and with all your soul, he will give the rain for
your land in its season, the early rain and the later rain, that
you may gather in your grain and your wine and your oil.
And he will give grass in your fields for your cattle, and you

---

3. See, for example, Deuteronomy 28:1–24; 7:12–24; 11:13–32.

shall eat and be full. Take heed lest your heart be deceived and you turn aside and serve other gods and worship them, and the anger of Yahweh be directed against you, and he shut the heavens, so that there will be no rain, and the land will yield no fruit, and you perish quickly off the good land which Yahweh gives you. (11:13–17)

But if you will not obey the voice of Yahweh your God or be careful to do all his commandments and his statutes which I command you this day, then all these curses shall come upon you and overtake you. Cursed shall you be in the city, and cursed shall you be in the field. Cursed shall be your basket and your kneading trough. Cursed shall be the fruit of your body and the fruit of your ground, the increase of your cattle and the young of your flock. Cursed shall you be when you come in, and cursed shall you be when you go out.

(28:15–19)

The conditions that regulate God's household are radically changed, indeed reconstituted, by Jesus' establishment of the kingdom of God in and through his ministry and finally through his death and resurrection. Membership is universalized and extended to all human beings. Hierarchy and patriarchy are abolished. The mediating activity of the priesthood and its temple cult as the broker between God as patron and Israel as client is canceled. Familyhood within this reconstituted household is organized horizontally. In Matthew's Gospel Jesus encloses all of his followers in the divine "I am" and shares with them "all authority in heaven and on earth."[4] In Luke's Acts of the Apostles all who belong to the new household of God receive the gift of the Holy Spirit and the divine affirmation of the tongue of fire. Empowered by the Spirit and authenticated as God's beloved daughters and sons, the members of this divine family live and act out of a consciousness of being co-enthroned with God and destined, like their Pioneer Jesus, to live forever and to participate in God's deity. That Spirit, which

---

4. This was already anticipated in Matthew 16:19, when Jesus bestowed on Simon Peter "the keys of the kingdom of the heavens."

"God sent into our hearts," authorizes the members of God's family of faith not only to call God *Abba* but also to embrace their new status of kings and queens who are "seated with Christ in the heavenly places" (Eph. 2:6) and therefore co-enthroned with God.

Abba is children's speech. It is the exclamatory form of address that Jewish children use to call their fathers from the time they learn to speak. It is an expression of intimacy and may be translated into English as "Papa" or "Daddy." This is the same form of address Jesus taught his disciples when he gave them the Lord's Prayer. The Lucan version of this prayer presents Jesus employing the Greek equivalent of the invocation *patêr*. But behind this simple title is the distinctive Aramaic appellation *abba* that was characteristic of Jesus' prayers, as Mark 14:36 indicates. Jesus wants his disciples to use the same title in order to give voice to the same familial and familiar relationship with God that he enjoys. For Jesus the fact of its masculine gender is meaningless. *Abba* has nothing to do with patriarchy. Its significance is intimacy. Its intent is to establish a bond of deep affection and familiarity between God, the founder of this family, and those who belong to it as God's beloved daughters and sons.

God, as the head of this household, continues to be named as father in the early Christian movement, but no longer in a hierarchical way as a patriarch. Jesus initiated a new form of address that the writings of the New Testament remotely echo, the Aramaic colloquial expression *Abba*. Although he employs the Greek word *patêr* in all four Gospels, except for that one instance in Mark 14:36, the equivalent in his mother tongue of Aramaic is not *abh* but *abba*. *Abh* would literally be translated into Greek as *patêr*.

Abba "had made considerable headway in Palestinian Aramaic in the period before the New Testament."[5] The

---

5. Joachim Jeremias, *The Prayers of Jesus*, Studies in Biblical Theology 6 (Naperville, Ill.: Alec R. Allenson, 1967), 58.

Targums, the Aramaic translation of the Hebrew Scriptures, bear witness to that development. Isaiah 8:4 uses *abba* ("Papa") and *imma* ("Mama") to replace *abhi* ("my father") and *immi* ("my mother") as the first words an infant would learn to speak. But children evidently did not stop addressing their parents as *abba* and *imma* when they became adults.[6] Isaac calls his father *abba* in Genesis 22:7, when he inquires about the lamb that is needed for the sacrifice Abraham is preparing, unaware that his father has been tempted to present him, Isaac, as an offering to God. Jacob addresses his father, Isaac, as *abba* when he, disguised as his brother Esau, approaches him with the savory dish of a goat disguised as venison in order to receive the blessing of the firstborn (Gen. 27:18). Joseph objects to his father giving the superior blessing to Ephraim instead of Manasseh: "Not so, *abba*, for this one [Manasseh] is the firstborn; put your right hand on his head" (Gen. 48:18). Jephthah is called *abba* by his daughter as she consents to serve as the sacrifice he offers to God for the victory he has gained over the Ammonites (Judg. 11:36). Finally, as Jesus testifies in Matthew 23:9, *abba* also appears to have been used as a respectful form of address for old men.

"In origin," according to Joachim Jeremias, "*abba* is a pure exclamatory form that is not inflected and that takes no possessive suffixes."[7] Because it also replaced the non-vocative use of *abhi* with its first person singular suffix, it can stand for "my father," or even "our father" and "his father."[8] Although there is an extensive employment of both forms in Palestinian Judaism before the time of Jesus, the use of *abba* is limited to fathers and old men. If Jeremias is right, "there is not a single instance of God being addressed

---

6. Ibid., 60; see also footnote 32 on page 58.
7. Ibid., 58.
8. Ibid., 59. This use of *abba* for "my father" also found its way into the Tannaitic writings of the Mishnah and the Tosephta.

as *abba* in Jewish prayers."[9] In view of the hierarchical structure of God's household to which both the Hebrew Scriptures and intertestamental Judaism attest, determined perhaps by the prevailing Mediterranean model of patron/client relationships, it would appear that such a form of address or even its nonvocative application to God would be regarded as irreverent and disrespectful.

Jesus, however, used *abba* in both ways: as an exclamatory form to address God and as a nonvocative form to speak about God. Only one Gospel text, Mark 14:36, has preserved an instance of the former: Jesus in Gethsemane calling upon God as *abba*.

> *Abba*, my Father *(ho patêr)*, all things are possible to you. Remove this cup from me; but not what I want but what you [want].

There are no occurrences of *abba* in the Gospels' perpetuation of Jesus' nonvocative references to God in his teaching. The Greek equivalent *patêr* or *ho patêr* has taken its place, and it is used at least 174 times: 4 in Mark, 42 in Matthew, 15 in Luke, and 109 in John. Twenty-one uses are encountered in prayers in which Jesus addresses God. The rest appear as references to God in Jesus' teaching. Not all of these occurrences, however, can be attributed to Jesus. Of the 42 in Matthew, 2 instances have been derived from Mark, 4 are in common with Luke; and of the 36 that are peculiar to Matthew, 4 have been introduced into traditions appropriated from Mark in which the word did not appear. These statistics and perhaps especially the 109 occurrences of the appellation "Father" in the Fourth Gospel reflect the growing tendency within the early church to multiply the title in the sayings of Jesus.[10] That would be the privilege of the Christian prophets speaking in the name of Jesus.

---

9. Ibid., 62.
10. These statistics are taken from ibid., 30–33.

The proliferation of this usage of Father in the Gospel tradition corresponds to the increasing naming of God as Father in the liturgy and catechetical instruction of the early church. The apostle Paul is not only the earliest witness to the use of *abba* in the Greek-speaking churches he founded; he himself has appropriated its Greek translation *patêr* and employs it twenty-four times in the seven letters that are generally attributed to his authorship. These are encountered in the liturgical phrases and prayers of his salutations, doxologies, benedictions, credal formulas, and prayers of thanksgiving and intercessions.

The New Testament writings of the first and second generations of the Christian movement, the letters of Paul as well as the four Gospels, evidence the widespread use of the title "Father" as a designation for God. Although the Greek form *patêr* is predominant, the three occurrences of *abba* in Galatians 4:6, Romans 8:15, and Mark 14:36 indicate that it was the original title that was employed in prayer and in references to God by Palestinian Jewish Christians. Because it is without parallel in the Hebrew Scripture and Palestinian Judaism, it earliest usage must be attributed to Jesus.

Undoubtedly *abba* is behind the Greek *patêr* that Jesus teaches his disciples in the Lucan version of the Lord's Prayer. Its use intimates a sense of immediate presence and presupposes intimacy, familiarity, and affection. Because Jesus has adopted children's speech, it might appear that the same hierarchical relationship is to be presupposed that required children to be subordinated to their father in a patriarchically structured society. The Gospel tradition, however, reflects a radically different relationship between Jesus and God. In his teaching and in his actions Jesus discloses an unprecedented authority that originates from his self-understanding of being co-enthroned with God and simultaneously called to serve as God's surrogate.

The table fellowship that Jesus inaugurates and promotes signifies the reconstituted household of God. It is inclusive, and it is also horizontally structured. All who are gathered around it and participate in its communion are the beloved sons and daughters of the mighty and eternal Creator who gave birth to them. They share the lordship which their Pioneer and Brother, Jesus, "the firstborn from the dead" (Rom. 8:29), has gained, and therefore they are sanctioned to understand themselves as being co-enthroned with him. With Jesus, therefore, they invoke their Parent Creator with the same degree of intimacy, familiarity, and affection that Jesus expressed in his employment of *abba*. Gender is immaterial. What matters is the affection, familiarity, and intimacy that arise from the self-understanding of those who identify themselves with this household and its founding Parent.

The expanded form of address in Matthew's version of the Lord's Prayer, however, reduces the immediate presence of God within this divine household: "Our Father, the One in the heavens." The possessive pronoun "our" stresses the communal relationship that the members of this family enjoy with the One who generated them. It reminds them that they all share the same generating Parent. But the sense of intimacy is diminished by emphasizing God's transcendence, by locating God "in the heavens."

"Heavenly Father" or "Father who is in heaven" are both vocative and nonvocative forms that are characteristic of Matthew's Gospel.[11] According to Jeremias, Johanan ben Zakkai, the founder of Rabbinic Judaism and a contemporary of the first generation of the Christian movement,

> seems to be the first to use the designation "heavenly Father" ("our heavenly Father," or "Israel's heavenly Father") for God.... Johanan may well have had a decisive influence in the introduction of the popular phrase into theological language. It certainly is not a coincidence that the considerable increase in the use of the designation "heavenly Father" in the tradition of the words of Jesus, as it is reflected in the Gospel of Matthew, comes at a time when Johanan was most

---

11. Matthew 5:48; 6:1, 14, 26, 32; 7:11, 21; 10:32–33; 12:50; 18:19; 23:9.

active (50–80); the tradition which Matthew took over was moulded in the decades before A.D. 80.[12]

However, as Jeremias also contends, "heavenly Father" did not become the predominant designation for God in Rabbinic Judaism.[13] That development appears to have been limited to the Evangelist Matthew and the community of his addressees. The general usage in the Christian movement seems to have preferred the plain appellation "Father." In the Gospel according to John, for example, Jesus refers to God as "Father" 109 times without ever prefixing it with the adjective "heavenly." God is designated "my Father" or "the Father." And when God is addressed by Jesus, the exclamatory form is the same as that which the Evangelist Mark (14:36) ascribes to Jesus in the prayer in Gethsemane: *abba* or "Father."[14]

The First Petition: Your Name Be Held in Awe

After the members of God's new household have invoked God as Papa or Father, the first petition they voice is "Your name be held in awe" or "Your name be reverenced." It is important to note that this petition is spoken in the third person imperative, and therefore it is not directed at God as an appeal. God is not being entreated to hallow God's own name. This is rather an exclamatory expression of the household's affirmation of the holiness of God's being.[15] After the Founder of this new household has been addressed intimately and familiarly as Papa or Father, it is appropriate and indeed necessary to acknowledge the wholly otherness and also the loftiness, the supremacy, and the sublimity of

---

12. Jeremias, *Prayers of Jesus*, 16–17.
13. Ibid., 17.
14. See John 17:1, 11, 24, 25; 11:41.
15. A current analogy would be the greeting "hail to the chief!" that someone might use in the presence of the president of the United States.

the Head of this family, none other than the Creator of the universe. Intimacy must not breed disrespect or contempt.

At the same time this employment of the third person imperative expresses the household's will that the name of God be reverenced or held in awe once and for all throughout the world. This also supports God's will as well as God's activity within the world to draw all human beings into this divine family in which God is loved and honored as the Creator who is engaged in drawing all humanity into a participation in God's kingdom, power, and glory.

"Your name be held in awe." But what is God's name? It cannot be God, for "God" is a common, not a proper, noun; and as a common noun it designates a class of beings or things. Does God have a name? Does God ever reveal a name by which God is to be identified? The first identity disclosed to Moses in the theophany at the blazing bush was "I am the God of your father, the God of Abraham, the God of Isaac, the God of Jacob." But apparently that self-identification was inadequate. Moses wanted to have a name by which God can be identified to the Hebrews in Egypt.

> If I come to the Israelites and say to them, "The God of your ancestors has sent me to you," and they ask me, "What is his name?" what shall I say to them? (Exod. 3:13)

God answers *ehyeh asher ehyeh*, a self-identification that is usually translated "I am who I am." Sometimes it is also rendered as "I will cause to be what I will cause to be." But the Hebrew verb *ehyeh* (a first person singular Qal future of the verb *hayyah*, meaning "to be") is more appropriately translated as "I will be."[16] Accordingly, God's self-identification to Moses is not to be construed as a name but rather as a notification that God cannot be confined by any name or title. That also holds true for God's correspond-

---

16. That is how it is translated by Robert C. Coote, *In Defense of Revolution: The Elohist History* (Minneapolis: Fortress, 1991), 41.

ing self-identification as Yahweh, a designation that is the third person singular of the same verb, *hayyah*.

> Thus you shall say to the Israelites, "Yahweh, the God of your ancestors, the God of Abraham, the God of Isaac, and the God of Jacob, has sent me to you: this is my name forever, and this my title for all generations." (Exod. 3:15)

While it may seem that Moses' request has been fulfilled by God's self-disclosure as Yahweh and by the solemn declaration "This is my name forever!" the word itself bears a meaning similar to that of the first person singular, "he who will be." God's selfhood cannot be expressed in a name. God is free to be what God will be, free to act in history as God wills. God's identity cannot be contained in a name.

Earlier in the Hebrew Scriptures, in Genesis 32:29, the patriarch Jacob, after having wrestled with God and having been renamed Israel, asks for God's name. But no name is given. Jacob's request is answered with the question "Why is it that you ask my name?" The refusal to divulge the name is based on the belief that knowledge of the name can yield effective power over the one who bears it. That is, a name is an identifier that makes it possible to differentiate, to order, to classify, and therefore also to limit. In Genesis 2:20 Adam names the animals God has created, and by ordering the creation he brings it under his control.

Nevertheless, in view of Yahweh's own avowal, "this is my name forever," the God of Israel was subsequently reverenced and worshiped by that name. According to the deuteronomistic historian and the Chronicler, Yahweh's dwelling place is in heaven, but at the same time Yahweh's name resides in the temple on earth.[17] Eventually the "name" Yahweh became so sacred and revered that it could no longer be spoken, and in time the correct pronunciation of its Hebrew form, YWHW, was lost. Circumlocutions like Adonai ("my Lord"), Shamaim ("heavens"), HaShem ("the Name"),

---

17. See 1 Kings 8:29, 43; 2 Chronicles 2:1–4; 6:10; 7:16, 20.

Elyonin ("Most High"), and Atiq Yomin ("the Ancient of Days") were substituted and by the time of Jesus were extensively employed as designations for God. Among them HaShem is especially significant in as far as it became a replacement for Yahweh. "The Name" and Yahweh are identical.

Accordingly, the petition "your name be held in awe" does not mean that the "name" Yahweh, which God disclosed to Moses, is to be hallowed. Nor does it imply that any other designations we might employ for the deity are to be kept sacred. There are no authentic names for God that are absolute and eternally valid. There are only metaphors and allusions, and none of them bear any finality. God discloses no other self-identification than "I will be who I will be"; and that is not a name but an advisement that the being of God cannot be captured or conveyed by any name or title. Behind the words "your name be held in awe" is the reality of the being of God, the Creator of the universe and the founding Parent of a divine family of humankind, and the reality of that Being is to be reverenced, glorified, and worshiped.

Chapter 6

The Second and Third Petitions

"Your rule come!"

"Your will be done, as in heaven also on earth."

Usually these petitions are differentiated from each other, and the latter, "Your will be done," is considered to be the third petition. But they are reciprocally related in meaning, and consequently they will be interpreted in relation to each other. God's rule and God's will are corresponding realities.

Like the previous petition, these two are formulated in the third person imperative. Therefore, they are not pleas addressed to God. They do not call upon God to establish God's rule or to implement God's will. God's kingdom has already come. God's will is already being done. The addressees of the two Gospels of Matthew and Luke, in which the Lord's Prayer is embedded, would have prayed these petitions fully aware of the inauguration of God's rule and the beginning of the fulfillment of God's will in and through the ministry of Jesus and finally through his death and resurrection. Accordingly, as a result of their interaction with his story as narrated by these Gospels, they would be inspired to extend these actualities in their own historical contexts by manifesting them in and through their deeds and words. Those who follow Jesus into death and resurrection and consequently allow themselves to be embraced by his "I with you am" (Matt. 28:20) are naturally drawn into those activities that belong to God's rule. Those who follow Jesus into death and resurrection and consequently receive the divine gifts of the Holy Spirit and the tongue of fire, according to Acts 2:3–4, naturally exercise their response-ability to fulfill God's will in their daily lives.

The Old Testament Background of the Kingdom of God

Jesus, as Matthew and Luke both testify, was completely committed to bringing about the long-awaited kingdom of God throughout his ministry. The Book of Daniel had envisioned this reality approximately 165 years before he was born. God's rule would be inaugurated after the present moral order was destroyed by a sudden, unexpected cataclysmic judgment of God. In the course of the history and experience of God's household of Israel the moral order of God's creation that extended back to the fall of Adam and Eve had reached a level of systemic evil and moral corruption that could no longer be reformed or rehabilitated. Human kingships had proven to be degenerate and inept in governing the people subject to their rule. They had failed to realize God's will for the creation, and their hierarchically constituted societies had not enabled their subjects to apprehend the promise and potentiality implied in being created in the likeness and image of God: to be "little less than God," to be "crowned with glory and honor," to exercise "dominion over the works of [God's] hands" and therefore also to enjoy the rights of autonomy and self-determination.[1]

The only recourse, according to the millennialism of Jewish apocalypticism, was divine deliverance into a new heaven and a new earth; that is, a new moral order in which God's rule would be established and justice and equality would prevail. That is the hope Daniel prophesied. That is the per-

---

1. See Psalm 8:3–8; Genesis 1:26–30.

spective similar millennial writings of apocalyptic Judaism expressed, and it may be represented as follows:

Creation (Gen. 1–2)	Divine Judgment	New Creation
	Dan. 2:36–45	
The Old Moral Order	Dan. 7:21–22	The New Moral Order

The beastly kingdoms and empires that "devoured much flesh" would be eradicated, and subsequently God would "set up a kingdom" on earth that would never be destroyed (Dan. 2:44–45). That kingdom would be a new moral order, and it would be placed under the jurisdiction of "one like a human being" who, according to Daniel's dream, would ascend into heaven on a cloud and receive from God "dominion, glory, and kingdom" (Dan. 7:13–14). This figure of the future, "one like a human being," is not an individual who may simply be identified with Jesus on the basis of his employment of the corresponding title "the Son of the Human Being." According to the exposition that the angelic interpreter communicates to Daniel, the "one like a human being" is a community.

> And the kingdom and the dominion and the greatness of the kingdoms under the whole heaven shall be given to the people of the saints of the Most High; their kingdom is an everlasting kingdom, and all dominions shall serve and obey them. (Dan. 7:27)

Jesus' Ministry as the Actualization of God's Rule

The phrases "the kingdom of God" and "the Son of Man" that are central to the preaching and teaching of Jesus in the Gospels of Matthew and Luke link Jesus to this tradition of Jewish millennialism. But it is his predecessor, John the Baptizer, who is representative of that tradition, not Jesus. In contrast Jesus not only proclaims the imminence of the new moral order of God's rule. He also brings it about through his activities of healing and teaching: "If by the finger of God I cast out demons, then the kingdom of God overtook you." Moreover, his ministry reflects a kingdom of God that is inclusive rather than exclusive. He does not separate the wheat from the chaff, the good from the evil. Instead he unites by drawing his fellow Jews back into the mainstream of society through exorcism, restoration, and forgiveness. Lepers are cleansed and returned to full membership in society. Men and women, segregated by the purity code of the law, are united in the communion of table fellowship with Jesus. The hemorrhaging woman (Matt. 9:20–22), who on the basis of Leviticus 15:19–30 has been ostracized from society for twelve years, is cured and restored to the fullness of life.[2] Sight and speech are given to the blind and the mute in order to enable them to enter more completely into community life and communication. The demon-possessed are liberated from their condition of living death and dehumanization. Even outsiders, like the centurion who represents the oppression of Rome or the Canaanite woman whose ancestors were dispossessed by the Israelites, are drawn into the benefits of God's rule through Jesus' healing of members of their household.

Jesus tells stories, indeed parables, in order to reveal to his contemporaries the revolutionary qualities of this kingdom that he is inaugurating. It is an indigenous reality that emerges and grows from the soil in which it was sown.[3] Like the vocation of agriculture, it includes both human and divine collaboration.[4] It is inclusive and does not practice separation before the final judgment of God.[5] It subverts

---

2. For a fuller exposition of the story of the hemorrhaging woman see Herman C. Waetjen, *The Origin and Destiny of Humanness: An Interpretation of the Gospel according to Matthew* (San Rafael, Calif.: Crystal Press, 1976), 125–26; also Herman C. Waetjen, *A Reordering of Power: A Sociopolitical Reading of Mark's Gospel* (Minneapolis: Fortress, 1989), 119–21.

3. The parable of the mustard seed in Matthew 13:31; see also Mark 4:30–32.

4. The parable of the seed growing secretly in Mark 4:26–29.

5. The parable of the wheat and the darnels in Matthew 13:24–30.

all purity codes[6] and systems of obligation.[7] It undermines honor/shame culture and its attendant patriarchal structures in order to liberate women as well as men from the oppressive order that is constituted.[8] It presupposes the integrity of uniting human identity and activity.[9] It is like a treasure hidden in a field for which a person will sell all possessions in order to enjoy all that can be acquired by its usability. At the same time it is like a priceless pearl for which a merchant will liquidate all his assets in order to possess it but will have nothing except the pearl.[10]

The similitude of the sower distinguishes Jesus' perspective of the kingdom of God from that of the apocalypticism of Daniel and other millennial writings.[11] Unlike many other parables, which are introduced by the phrase "the kingdom of God is like," the similitude of the sower has no referent. Nevertheless, it may safely be assumed that its referent is identical to that of the other parables. Accordingly, "the kingdom of God is like a sower who went out to sow." That is, God's rule is like an agricultural season. In contrast to the apocalyptic outlook, a new heaven and a new earth are not created by God after the old moral order has been destroyed by a sudden, unexpected cataclysmic event of divine judgment. In its likeness to an agricultural season, God's rule is like grain that is sown into the earth and, during its subsequent period of growth, encounters the contingencies of agricultural realities. There is much loss along the way. At the time of sowing the farmer experiences the first setback: birds that gobble up the seeds that have not been covered with soil in the process of plowing. The second loss occurs when the young shoots of grain are unable to penetrate more

---

6. The parables of the good Samaritan and the great banquet in Luke 10:25–37; 14:16–24.

7. The parable of the unmerciful servant in Matthew 18:23–35.

8. The parable of the widow and the judge in Luke 18:2–5.

9. The parable of the ten virgins in Matthew 25:1–13.

10. The parables of the treasure and the pearl in Matthew 13:44–46.

11. The parable of the sower in Matthew 13:3–9; see also Mark 4:3–9.

deeply into the rocky soil for moisture and nutrients, and therefore they are scorched by the sun. Later in the agricultural season the grain is overwhelmed by the vigorous growth of competing weeds. Only at harvest time does the gain that the seed has succeeded in producing become evident; and, according to Jesus' parable, the gain more than offsets the loss that has been incurred.[12]

Unquestionably the distinctive character and content of Jesus' career diverge significantly from the tradition of Jewish millennialism as well as the correlative activity of John the Baptizer. Unlike John, Jesus does not wait for God's rule to come. In and through his activities of teaching and healing he makes present the new moral order that is anticipated as a future reality. He begins to embody the "one like a human being" (Dan. 7:13) as the Son of Man. Accordingly, the eschatological perspective of Jesus' inauguration of God's rule in time and history, as it is reflected in the narrative worlds of Matthew and Luke, may be represented as follows:

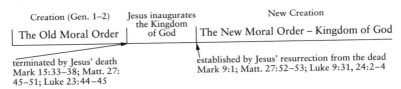

The old moral order, which was introduced by the fall of Adam and Eve, has continued through the time of Jesus into the present. The human infection of sin as it manifests itself in unlimited means and ways in human relationships and cultural institutions is apparent to everyone. What is not so conspicuous is the reality of God's rule that Jesus inaugurated and that God established once and for all through the resurrection of Jesus from the dead. However, even if it is not visible to sense experience, it is nevertheless a con-

---

12. See Waetjen, *A Reordering of Power*, 100–103.

cealed actuality. Therefore it must be incarnated in deeds and actions similar to those that the Gospels attribute to Jesus' ministry in order to make it, the new moral order of God's rule, empirically perceptible.

The kingdom of God has come, although not in its fullness. The reality of God's rule continues to be like an agricultural season. That season has continued into the present and may extend far into the future before the harvest, the parousia or the so-called second coming of the Son of Man, takes place. For although the old moral order persists into the present, it is gradually being subverted and superseded by the new moral order of the kingdom of God. And if that is not discernibly happening, it is because the contemporary disciples of Jesus are not aware that God's rule has been placed under their jurisdiction and that they have been mandated to authenticate it, to make it visible in their social relationships and vocational activity.

For parallel to the figure of "one like a human being" (Dan. 7:13), to whom "dominion, glory, and kingdom" are given, "the Son of the Human Being" or preferably the new Human Being of the Gospels is a corporate reality, indeed, "the saints of the Most High." Jesus, of course, is the originator of this community. He is first and foremost the new Human Being. But his disciples, who have followed him into God's rule, are members of this corporate reality. With Jesus they constitute God's reconstituted household. The response-ability of incarnating and expanding this household of God's rule beyond Jesus' death and resurrection has been handed over to them. As Jesus said at the Passover in the Lucan context of the institution of the Eucharist:

> I assign to you as my father assigned to me a kingdom, so that you may eat and drink at my table in my kingdom. (Luke 22:29–30a)

To fulfill that response-ability of incarnating and expanding God's rule, the disciples are empowered by the Holy

Spirit to continue Jesus' ministry of proclaiming the Good News of God's rule and manifesting it through their work of healing and exorcism (Matt. 10:1; Luke 9:1–2). Central to their training for the mission of expanding the kingdom of God are the glimpses of phenomenal possibility that Jesus discloses to them by his mighty works of stilling the storm, feeding the multitudes, and participating in the sovereignty of God by walking on the Sea of Galilee. Their membership in the new household of God's rule and their empowerment by God's indwelling Spirit predestine them to participate in God's sovereignty and to realize comparable possibilities.

God's family conducts God's rule as a present reality on God's behalf. This is an essential feature of the distinctive consciousness and sense of self-understanding that is to be presupposed for the praying of this petition "Your rule come." The members of God's household know that it has come. They continue to experience its reality in their lives. They are engaged in incarnating it through their deeds and words. But they also know that it is by no means a consummated reality in which all human beings participate; and therefore they pray "Your rule come" in the aorist imperative in order to express the ultimate will and purpose of God. That is: Your kingdom come once and for all!

This petition, as already indicated, is formulated in the third person imperative and therefore is not an appeal to God. It expresses the household's affirmation and support of God's activity in the world: activity in which the household itself participates as the present bearer of God's rule, activity that is directed at culminating God's rule in the world by drawing all human beings into the "I am" of the resurrected Jesus of Nazareth. When that objective has been reached, "God will have become all things in all things" (1 Cor. 15:28); and at long last God's will and purpose will have been finalized.

The Third Petition: Your Will Be Done, As in Heaven Also on Earth

This perspective on the present and future reality of God's rule tends to make the third petition superfluous, for it is an extension of the household's exclamation that the kingdom of God be fully and finally inaugurated. Since it appears only in Matthew's expanded version of the Lord's Prayer, it may be an elaboration attributable to the Evangelist himself or, what is more likely, an enlargement that originated in the worship and liturgical practice of Matthew's church.[13] Perhaps it was drawn from the prayer that Jesus voiced in Gethsemane as he confronted his forthcoming passion:

> My Father, if it is possible, let this cup pass from me; but not as I will, but as you will. (Matt. 26:39)

Like the previous petitions, this third petition is spoken in the third person imperative. In a similar manner it voices the household's summons of the fulfillment of God's will on earth, while it simultaneously presupposes the household's own involvement in the fulfillment of that will. In Matthew's Gospel Simon Peter, serving as the representative and spokesman of God's household, is entrusted with "the keys of the kingdom of God." Accordingly, he and all those whom he represents are appointed to serve as bearers of the authority of God's rule.

> whatever you bind on earth will be bound in heaven, and whatever you loose on earth will be loosed in heaven.
> (Matt. 16:19)

The authority that the keys grant is the privilege of dispensing the riches of God's rule throughout the world. It is also the prerogative of determining ethical conduct and community practice by establishing or dissolving institutional

---

13. Joachim Jeremias, *The Prayers of Jesus*, Studies in Biblical Theology 6 (Naperville, Ill.: Alec R. Allenson, 1967), 89.

structures, precedents and programs, creeds and codes according to human need. The freedom to exercise the keys is unqualified. Heaven, that is, God, will validate the exercise of this divine authority and its resulting judgments and determinations. Using the keys to promote the growth and expansion of God's rule is, therefore, a fulfillment of God's will.

God's will on earth is ultimately the triumph of God's rule. Insofar as the members of God's new household are fulfilling their response-ability in bringing about God's rule through their deeds and words, God's will is being done. However, God's sons and daughters are united with their founding Parent in yearning for the consummation of God's will that will terminate the realities of evil, death, injustice, oppression, suffering, pain, and crying. For the former things will have passed away, and all humanity will be participating in the transcendence and transfiguration that Jesus disclosed during his ministry.

> Then the just will shine as the sun in the kingdom of their Father. (Matt. 13:43)

Chapter 7

The Fourth Petition

*"Keep on giving us each day the bread
for our existence."*

"Give us today the bread for our existence."

The previous petitions have been spoken in the third person imperative. They are not requests or pleas addressed to God. Instead they are the household's endorsements of God's activities. Through Jesus Christ God has inaugurated the kingdom. God's will is in the process of being fulfilled. Those who pray these petitions, namely, the members of God's household, are currently engaged in exercising and expanding God's rule and the realization of God's will. As collaborators with God, therefore, they are summoning the consummation of God's design for the creation.

Now, for the first time in the Lord's Prayer, the second person imperative is used: "[You] keep on giving" (Luke 11:3) or "[You] give" (Matt. 6:11). God is being addressed directly; indeed God is being commanded.

But while both Lucan and Matthean versions of this petition agree in the usage of the second person imperative, they diverge in the choice of tense as well as in other ways. Luke's formulation employs the imperative in the present tense, signifying continuous action: keep on giving. Matthew's version is expressed in the aorist tense, denoting a single action and therefore perhaps representing a command to give instantly, even with a sense of urgency. Or it may convey the limited time factor: give today.

73

Which of the two versions might be considered to be the more original? The difficulty is not easy to resolve, and convincing arguments can be made for both. Joachim Jeremias conjectures that the Matthean formulation of the petition with its use of the aorist imperative *(dos)* is the original because all the other petitions of the Lord's Prayer are voiced in the aorist tense.[1] But such a production of parallelism, as he argues earlier, is characteristic of liturgical usage.[2] That is, a tradition, like the Lord's Prayer, that is consistently used in public worship and in personal devotion may be expanded and elaborated; but at the same time it will also be stylized and standardized. Accordingly, it would seem that the Lucan formulation is earlier. The liturgical effect of parallelism has not yet converted the present imperative into an aorist imperative so that the tense of this petition would correspond stylistically to the use of the aorist in the other petitions.

But the change in wording at the conclusion of this petition must also be taken into account. Luke ends it with the prepositional phrase "each day," and therefore the corresponding employment of the present imperative is appropriate. For, if the plea is for bread each day, the imperative necessarily must express continuous giving: "Keep on giving us bread... each day."

Matthew's version corresponds to the subsequent exhortations of Jesus in the Sermon on the Mount: "Don't be anxious about your life, what you will eat or what you will drink," and "don't be anxious for tomorrow" (Matt. 6:25, 34). Consequently the petition ends with the adverb "today."[3] If the disciples are not to worry about what they will eat and drink tomorrow, then this petition must be limited

---

1. Joachim Jeremias, *The Prayers of Jesus*, Studies in Biblical Theology 6 (Naperville, Ill.: Alec R. Allenson, 92. Jeremias is arguing here against the perspective he expressed on page 90.

2. Ibid., 90.

3. Luke does not present Jesus exhorting his disciples, "Don't be anxious for tomorrow." However, what Jesus teaches in Matthew 6:25–33 appears in Luke 12:22–31.

to praying for bread only for today. Accordingly, the aorist tense of the imperative mood is appropriate to Matthew's rendering of this petition.

The Problematic Word *Epioúsion* in This Petition

A more troublesome difficulty is the meaning of *epioúsion*, a word not found in Greek before its occurrence in both the Lucan and Matthean versions of this petition. The fifth edition of Walter Bauer's *Greek-English Lexicon of the New Testament and Other Early Christian Literature*, revised and augmented in a second edition by F. W. Gingrich and F. W. Danker, acknowledges the judgment of Origen, the great Alexandrian and Caesarean scholar of the third century, that the word was coined by the Evangelists. Origen himself treated it as a combination of two words, *epí* ("for") and *ousía* ("being"), and translated it "necessary for existence."[4] Most English translations, however, render it "daily" by reducing *epioúsion* to three words, *epí* ("for"), *tên* ("the"), and *oúsan* ("being"), and adding, as though understood, *hêméran* ("day"); in other words, "for the current day."

Sometimes a footnote is included which offers the phrase "for tomorrow" as an alternative rendering. This is based on Jerome's observation, recorded in his notes on the Gospel according to Matthew, that the wording of this petition in the Aramaic version of the Lord's Prayer in the lost Jewish-Christian Gospel of the Nazarenes was *mahar*, which means "tomorrow." *Mahar*, however, reflects the eschatology of the Palestinian Jewish-Christian community, whose interpretation of the Easter event was determined by an Elijah or a Moses typology. God's act of raising Jesus from the dead

---

4. See F. W. Gingrich and F. W. Danker, second revised and augmented edition of Walter Bauer's fifth edition of *A Greek-English Lexicon of the New Testament and Other Early Christian Literature* (Chicago: University of Chicago Press, 1979), 296–97.

signaled only the beginning of a new exodus. Like his pre-
decessors, Elijah and Moses, Jesus was assumed into heaven
and, as the fulfillment of Deuteronomy 18:15, he is to be
distinguished as the last prophet of the old moral order.
Through his spokespersons on earth he will conduct God's
people into the new promised land. When that goal is finally
reached, the rule of God will be actualized, and Jesus will
then be revealed as the Messiah.[5]

Nevertheless, Jeremias argues for this translation of *epioúsion* and justifies it by correlating it with the meals that Jesus
shared with his disciples.

> Every meal his disciples had with him was a usual eating
> and drinking, and yet it was more: a meal of salvation, a
> messianic meal, image and anticipation of the meal at the
> consummation, because he was the master of the house. This
> remained true in the primitive church: their daily fellowship
> meals were the customary meals for sustenance, and yet at
> the same time they were a "Lord's supper" (1 Cor. 11:20)
> which mediated fellowship with him and linked in fellowship
> with one another those sitting at table (1 Cor. 10:16f.).[6]

In other words, this petition has a predominantly future orientation. While it is an entreaty for physical sustenance for
today, it is simultaneously a plea for the "bread of the age of
salvation." Accordingly, he translates the petition "Give us
today the bread for tomorrow."

But the rule of God has been inaugurated. The future has
become present. The bread of tomorrow is already here. The
reality of the age of salvation is not to be projected into the
future, nor is it to be relegated to a transcendent realm that
exists alongside of the old moral order but does not participate in it.[7] God's rule has not yet been consummated, and the

---

5. See Acts 3:17–26; 6:1–6. For a portrayal of this Palestinian Jewish-Christian
community and the differences between it and the Hellenistic Jewish-Christian community, see Philip F. Esler, *Community and Gospel in Luke-Acts: The Social and
Political Motivations of Lucan Theology* (New York: Cambridge University Press,
1987), 71–109.

6. Jeremias, *Prayers of Jesus*, 102.

7. Ibid. 101–2. Jeremias appears to contradict himself. He insists that the peti-

fullness of salvation has not yet been attained. The old moral order continues to dominate the world and to obstruct the realization of God's will. Nevertheless, God's reconstituted household is an actuality in the world; and God's adults, as bearers of the Holy Spirit, are commissioned and empowered to pursue the extension of God's rule until its objectives of worldwide liberation, justice, and peace have been achieved. And while they are fulfilling their mission, these daughters and sons of this divine household are being nourished with the bread of life through community relationships, worship, the proclamation of the Word, and the celebration of the Eucharist.

Although Jerome noted that the Aramaic vocable *mahar* was used in the petition for bread in the Gospel of the Nazarenes, he did not accept this as an equivalent of the distinctive Greek term *epioúsion*. While the earlier versions of the Old Latin had rendered it as *quotidianus* ("daily"), he translated it literally with the Latin compound *super-substantialis*, that is, "supersubstantial." The Sinaitic and Curetonian versions of the Syriac translation of the Lord's Prayer use *amina*, meaning "continual," but the Peshitta Syriac prefers *desunkanan* ("for our need"). Origen's analysis of the word is close to the translation of the Peshitta. Given the uniqueness of the term, which is found only two or three times after its use in Matthew and Luke, it would appear that the ancients who translated the Greek text of the petition into Latin or Syriac or who attempted to explain the word guessed at its meaning.

Is it possible to determine the sense of *epioúsion*? Since it is used in both versions of this petition, it must bear a meaning that is conducive to both. At least the futuristic sense of "tomorrow" may be ruled out initially on the basis of the

---

tion for the "bread for tomorrow" does not sever everyday life and the kingdom of God from one another. Yet he claims that our world is "enslaved under Satan" and "God is remote." If the former view is correct and the rule of God is a present reality, then God cannot be remote; and the Holy Spirit is in the process of "proving the world wrong about sin and righteousness and judgment" (John 16:8).

witness of the Gospels to the establishment of the new moral
order of God's rule and its transfer from Jesus to his community of the new humanity.[8] Consequently, it would appear
that only the remaining two possible meanings of *epioúsion*
are credible: "daily" and "necessary for our existence"; that
is, "Keep on giving us our daily bread" and "Keep on giving
us the bread necessary for our existence."

But which of the two may be regarded as the essential
meaning of *epioúsion?* A decoding of the component units
of the word makes both seem equally valid:

> *epi tên ousan* and supplying *hêmeran:* "for the current day"
> or "daily"

> *epi ousia:* "for being," "for existence," or "necessary for
> existence"

Ultimately it may not matter which is more accurate. Both
are meaningful in their own right. Yet the latter is appeal-
ing, for it can be argued that *epioúsion* is equivalent to the
Targum rendering of Proverbs 30:8:

> give me neither poverty nor riches; feed me with *lachma
> misati.*

Literally translated, *lachma misati* means "bread, my required portion." In other words, this unusual Greek term
may be a translation of the Aramaic vocable *misati* ("required portion") and therefore may bear a corresponding meaning.[9] "Keep on giving us the required portion of
bread," that is, the "bread necessary for our existence." If
this is the case, the meaning of *epioúsion* seems to have been
surmised correctly by Origen and the translator of the Syriac
Peshitta.

---

8. Luke 12:32; 22:29; Matthew 28:16–20. See also above pp. 35–36, 42.

9. Arnold Meyer, *Jesu Muttersprache* (Freiburg: J. C. B. Mohr [Paul Siebeck],
1896), 107–8, offers an investigation of this Greek term by attempting to recover
the Aramaic original that Jesus may have used and concludes that "necessary for
existence" is the more correct meaning. Matthew Black, *An Aramaic Approach
to the Gospels and Acts*, 2d ed. (Oxford: Clarendon Press, 1954),149–53, prefers
yoma den weyomachra ("day by day") as the original Aramaic phrase that Jesus
employed. I found Meyer more convincing.

Matthew's version of the petition limits the plea for bread to today: "Give us today the bread necessary for our existence." Because this rendering seems to be determined by Jesus' subsequent exhortation to his disciples in 6:34 not to be anxious about tomorrow, it would appear that the Lucan formulation is probably the more original of the two. Its use of the present tense of the imperative, "keep on giving," obviously implies God's sustained provision of bread required for the sustenance of this divine household Jesus is constituting. Such reliability is both affirmed and invoked by this purposeful employment of the present imperative. Moreover, the underlying experience of dependability, which this petition intimates, certifies the continuous reliance of this community on God's faithfulness.

Praying This Petition from the Perspective of Continued Participation in the Old Moral Order

Insofar as the members of this household are also involved in the old moral order and therefore subjected to the economic and political forces of a hierarchically controlled society as well as the contingencies of nature, their limited power and autonomy will not guarantee the continuous provision of "required bread" or bread necessary for their well-being. In spite of their efforts, unemployment, physical disabilities, sickness, death of the breadwinner, and even persecution may prevent them from maintaining their livelihood. Additionally, the stark realities of war, drought, famine, and disease pose a continuous threat to the adequacy of their food supply.

Consequently, while the sons and daughters of this household are engaged in administering God's rule and doing God's work, God, as the Head of this household, must supply their physical needs day by day. That is precisely what God has been doing, as the Lucan formulation of this petition implies. Accordingly, the Lucan community is being taught to express its continued reliance on God's dependability: "Keep on giving us the bread necessary for our existence."

Matthew's addressees, who enjoy wealth and its advantages, are charged:

> Do not be anxious about your life, what you will eat or what you will drink, nor for your body, what you will wear.... First look for the kingdom and its justice, and all these things will be added to you. Therefore do not be anxious for tomorrow, for tomorrow will be anxious for itself. Enough for a day is its own evil. (6:33–34)

In accordance with this instruction, the petition they are to pray is "Give us today the bread necessary for our existence." Like the Israelites in the wilderness after the great Exodus from Egypt, they are to live confidently that their Father in heaven will provide the basic necessities of life for them, but day by day (see Exod. 16:4–21).

Holy Bread

The material bread that God provides for the members of this divine household is holy bread. It is holy because God gives it. It is holy because Jesus sanctified it at the Passover celebration of the Exodus when he took the bread of the meal, blessed and broke it, and gave it to his disciples to symbolize the corporate reality of his body and their participation in it (Luke 22:19). It is holy because on Easter evening, in and through his act of blessing and breaking bread, the two disciples of Emmaus recognized him and correspondingly became aware of their own membership in the new creation that he embodied (Luke 24:30–31). It is holy because it will be eaten by those who are holy as "saints of the Most High" who embrace their identity as God's beloved daughters and sons.

There is one bread, as the apostle Paul enunciates, "and we who are many are one body, for we all partake of one bread"(1 Cor. 10:17). Therefore, this petition for material bread does not negate the symbolic significance attributed to bread in the New Testament. While it is material bread necessary for daily existence, it is at the same time spiritual bread, the Bread of Life. As it sustains physical life, it reminds those who receive it of those who are still hungry and poor as a result of unemployment, homelessness, racism, famine, and disease. As it sustains physical life, it symbolizes the inextricable union of all those who partake of it with the rest of humanity, those who are still entrapped in the old moral order as well as those who are fellow members of God's new household of faith.

Chapter 8

The Fifth Petition

"And forgive us our sins, for we ourselves also forgive everyone owing us."

"And forgive us our debts, as we also have forgiven our debtors."

This fifth petition, like the fourth, employs the second person imperative: "[you] forgive." God is again being addressed with an appeal. As previously, God is being commanded. But unlike the foregoing petitions, the fifth begins with the conjunction "and," which joins this entreaty to the preceding one and binds them together. In both the Matthean and Lucan versions the conjunction is placed between the two petitions:

> Give us today the bread necessary for our existence, and forgive us our debts, as we also have forgiven our debtors. (Matt. 6:11–12)

> Keep on giving us each day the bread necessary for our existence, and forgive us our sins, for we ourselves also forgive everyone owing us. (Luke 11:3–4a)

The implication is that the two petitions are interdependent and therefore are to be comprehended in relation to each other. This, however, is truer of the Matthean than the Lucan version, because, as will become evident, its formulation remains within the framework of indebtedness: "forgive us our debts *(opheilēmata)*, as we forgive our debtors *(opheiletais)*." The Lucan version, *hamartias*

82

("sins"), may be due to the adaptation of the petition to Greco-Roman addressees, who likely would not understand the Jewish conception of debt. Yet strikingly the Lucan construction does not remain within the framework of sins but concludes the petition with a reorientation toward indebtedness: "forgive us our sins, for we ourselves forgive everyone owing *(opheilonti)* us." That makes it likely that the term "debts" belonged to the earliest wording of the petition.[1] Consequently it would seem that in this case the Matthean version is more original than the Lucan.[2]

There are other significant differences in the two versions, particularly in the second half of the petition. The Lucan formulation follows the use of the aorist imperative, "[you] forgive," with the present indicative of the same verb, "we forgive" introduced by the causal conjunction "for" and adding the reflexive pronoun "ourselves": "for we ourselves also forgive." God is being entreated to forgive because we are forgiving others. If the presumption of this imperative addressed to God is the expectation of forgiveness, the only appropriate presupposition on the part of the one praying this petition must be identical conduct. The members of God's household are commanding their founding Parent to close the past so that it will not affect their mutual relationship in the present or the future. At the same time, they are acting in this way in their relationship to each other as well as to those outside of their household. All retaliation is renounced. Forgiveness extinguishes the "spirit of vengeance." The freedom of God, which is an essential reality of this household, requires of those who participate in it nothing less than this mutuality of forgiving.

The same holds true for the Matthean formulation of this petition. Following the aorist imperative, "[you] forgive

---

1. Joachim Jeremias, *The Prayers of Jesus,* Studies in Biblical Theology 6 (Naperville, Ill.: Alec R. Allenson, 92. Jeremias is arguing here against the perspective he expressed on page 90.
2. Ibid.

our sins," the adverbial conjunction *hôs* ("as") introduces a comparison in which the main verb is expressed in the perfect indicative: "we have forgiven." The entreaty intends to convey to God that the members of this divine household have been forgiving debts and therefore are living in unobligedness from the past into the present. Moreover, the implication is that they will continue to do so into the future. Correspondingly, even as they in their freedom engage in forgiving others and thereby give evidence of their membership in God's family, they are entitled to command God to forgive them.

The petition, therefore, in both its Lucan and Matthean versions, implies that those whom God has generated and who therefore belong to God's household will act like their divine Parent and be true to their identity as God's sons and daughters. Jesus, in his teaching, exhorted his disciples to incarnate such a disposition:

> Be perfect, therefore, as your heavenly Father is perfect.
>
>   (Matt. 5:48)

> Be compassionate, even as your Father is compassionate.
>
>   (Luke 6:36)

The only obligation imposed on those who identify themselves with God's family is to be predisposed to imitating God. Integrity is the essential mark or stamp of this divine household. Consequently, the ongoing practice of forgiving others qualifies its members for God's forgiveness. But if they cannot forgive, they have violated their own integrity and negated their identity as members of God's household. As a result, they have forfeited God's forgiveness of their own sins. For, as Jesus proceeds to tell his disciples after teaching them the Lord's Prayer:

> If you forgive human beings their transgressions, your heavenly Father will also forgive you; but if you do not forgive human beings, neither will your Father forgive your transgressions. (Matt. 6:14–15)

Debts and Debtors

The Matthean version of this fifth petition, however, focuses on debts and debtors, not transgressions or sins, and this bears a distinctively Jewish perspective. The reality of indebtedness is a fundamental human condition resulting from being nurtured, made morally aware, and being enabled to actualize one's potentiality within and by a community. But for Judaism and for earlier Israelite religion indebtedness was determined by the entry into a covenantal relationship with Yahweh. The Book of Deuteronomy expresses this binding reality forcefully:

> But it is because Yahweh loves you and is keeping the oath which he swore to your fathers that Yahweh has brought you out with a mighty hand and redeemed you from the house of bondage, from the hand of Pharaoh king of Egypt.... You shall therefore be careful to do the commandment, and the statutes, and the ordinances, which I command you this day. And because you hearken to these ordinances and keep and do them, Yahweh your God will keep with you the covenant and the steadfast love which he swore to your fathers to keep. He will love you, bless you, and multiply you; he will also bless the fruit of your body and the fruit of your ground, your grain and your wine and your oil, the increase of your cattle and the young of your flock, in the land which he swore to your fathers to give you. You shall be blessed above all peoples; there shall not be male or female barren among you or among your cattle. And Yahweh will take away from you all sickness; and none of the evil diseases of Egypt, which you knew, will he inflict upon you, but he will lay them on all who hate you. (Deut. 7:8, 11–15)

But if you will not obey the voice of Yahweh your God or be careful to do all his commandments and his statutes which I command you this day, then all these curses shall come upon you and overtake you. Cursed shall you be in the city, and cursed shall you be in the field. Cursed shall be your basket and your kneading trough. Cursed shall be the fruit of your body and the fruit of your ground, the increase of your cattle and the young of your flock. Cursed shall you be when you

come in, and cursed shall you be when you go out. Yahweh
will send upon you curses, confusion, and frustration in all
that you undertake to do, until you are destroyed and perish
quickly, on account of the evil of your doings, because you
have forsaken me. Yahweh will make the pestilence cleave
to you until he has consumed you off the land which you
are entering to take possession of it. Yahweh will smite you
with consumption and with fever, inflammation, and fiery
heat, and with drought, and with blasting, and with mildew;
they shall pursue you until you perish. And the heavens over
your head shall be brass, and the earth under you shall be
iron. Yahweh will make the rain of your land powder and
dust; from heaven it shall come down upon you until you are
destroyed. (Deut. 28:15–24)

Reciprocity and obligation characterize this covenantal relationship between Yahweh and Israel in the Old Testament.
Yahweh delivered Israel from Egyptian enslavement, and Israel, by entering into a covenant with Yahweh, has been
established as Yahweh's household. As the patriarch of this
household, Yahweh makes its members morally aware by imposing his rules and regulations upon them. By living and
acting within this network of obligations, Israel is not only
nurtured and cared for but also guaranteed a future. In reciprocity Yahweh enables Israel to realize its great potentiality
as the household of God.

In contrast, the new household of God that Jesus constitutes and that God authenticates by resurrecting Jesus from
the dead is characterized by unobligedness. Reciprocity has
been canceled by "that appropriate death which brings to
an end an appropriate mode of discharging one's obligations."[3] That appropriate death is the death of Jesus and
his disciples' participation in it. Accordingly, covenantal indebtedness has been superseded by a covenant of grace and
freedom. Forgiveness is now unlimited in the new moral
order of God's rule. "How often shall my brother [or sister]

---

3. Kenelm Burridge, *New Heaven-New Earth: A Study of Millenarian Activities*
(New York: Schocken, 1969), 6.

sin against me and I forgive him [her]? Seven times?" Peter asks in Matthew's discourse on community life and relationships (18:21). "I say to you, not seven times but seventy times seven," Jesus replies (18:22). The integrity of God's daughters and sons requires the unlimited remission of all indebtedness in emulation of God's infinite forgiveness.

The Parable of the Unforgiving Slave

Jesus' parable of the unforgiving slave illustrates this reality of unlimited forgiveness and simultaneously subverts the deuteronomistic ideology of covenantal reciprocity.

> The rule of the heavens is like a king who wished to settle an account with his slaves. Now as he began to reckon, one debtor of myriads of talents was brought before him. Since he could not repay, the master commanded that he be sold along with his wife and children and all his possessions, and [thereby he, the master] be repaid. Then falling, the slave bowed before him saying, "Have patience with me, and I will repay you everything." And being moved with compassion the master of that slave released him and forgave him the debt. Now going out that slave found one of his fellow slaves who owed him one hundred denarii, and, seizing him, he began to choke him saying, "Repay what you owe!" Then falling, his fellow slave was begging him saying, "Have patience with me, and I will repay you." But he was not willing, and, going off, he threw him into prison until he repaid what he owed. Therefore, his fellow slaves, seeing the things that had happened, were greatly distressed and going reported to their master all the things that had happened. Then his master, summoning him, says to him, "Wicked slave, that entire debt I forgave you, since you implored me. Was it not necessary that you also show mercy on your fellow slave, as I showed mercy on you?" And being angry his master handed him over to the torturers until he repaid all that he owed him. So also my heavenly Father will do to you, if each of you do not forgive his [her] brother [sister] from your heart.
>
> (Matt. 18:23–35)

The world of Jesus' story is a royal court at which slaves are being challenged to account for their contractual guaranty of assessed tax income. Although they are designated slaves, they are tax farmers who through competitive bidding have gained the privilege of collecting the royal tribute in the imperial provinces of the empire. Vast sums of money are involved. The first slave or tax farmer owes the royal treasury "myriads of talents." One talent amounts to approximately sixty-five pounds of silver and is the equivalent of six thousand denarii or the wage of six thousand days of labor. A myriad is ten thousand, the highest number in the Greek vocabulary. But the indebtedness is stipulated as "myriads of talents," or sixty-five pounds of silver times ten thousand times ten thousand.[4] An incalculable sum, a sum as large as the annual budget of the Roman Empire, if not larger! It is probably an exaggerated image intended to convey the impossibility of the slave's capability to repay in spite of his pledge: "Have patience with me, and I will repay you everything."

Unexpectedly the king's threat to have the slave, his family, and his possessions sold as punishment is not carried out. The first scene of the story ends with a stunning climax of forgiveness, the remission of the entire debt. Through the king's compassion the slave has become unobliged.

The second scene is equally surprising. The forgiven slave refuses to conduct his subsequent life and relationships on the basis of the unobligedness he has experienced. He seizes a fellow tax farmer by the throat and demands the repayment of the owed sum of one hundred denarii; when the fellow tax farmer is unable to repay, he has him thrown into debtor's prison until the debt is repaid. The slave is unable to behave like the king.

---

4. See Marvin A. Powell, "Weights and Measures," in *The Anchor Dictionary of the Bible*, ed. David Noel Freedman (New York: Doubleday, 1992), 6:907. Powell calculates "at least 204 metric tons of silver...the fabulous sum of 60 million denarii."

The third scene presents the tragic conclusion of the story. The fellow slaves are outraged by the injustice that the first slave has perpetrated and report the matter to the king. Brought back into the royal court for a new reckoning, the unmerciful slave is condemned by the king, "Was it not necessary that you show mercy to your fellow slave as I showed mercy to you?" As punishment, the original debt is reinstated, and the slave is delivered to the torturers (sometimes translated "jailers") to determine if and where some of that tax revenue might have been concealed and perhaps also to extort much of the owed amount from friends and relatives.

The fantastic amount of the first slave's debt corresponds metaphorically to the indebtedness of human beings to God their Creator for the incalculable gift of life and the possibilities of self-realization that accompany it. Such a vast debt would naturally evoke obligation as an existential condition. Moreover, that obligation would be reinforced within Israelite religion and Judaism by the remembrance and celebration of God's deliverance from Egyptian enslavement and the attendant covenantal promises of the fullness of life and the realization of wonderful possibilities. The Book of Deuteronomy, as already observed, is the classic biblical expression of this ideology of reciprocity.

But in contrast to most, if not all, the kings of history, this regent forgives the slave's enormous debt, a debt that could hardly be repaid in a lifetime, and sets the slave free to live without the burden of obligation. That is the grace of the new covenant. But unobligedness may also be a burden that is difficult to bear, especially if it is an existential condition. Nothing less than the freedom of unobligedness, however, characterizes the new household of God. To the host who had invited him to a banquet Jesus said,

> When you make a noon meal or a dinner, do not invite your friends or your brothers [or sisters] or your kinsfolk or your rich neighbors, lest they invite you back and it becomes a repayment to you. But when you make a banquet, invite the

destitute, the crippled, the lame, the blind, and you will be blessed because they do not have [anything] to repay you. For it will be repaid to you in the resurrection of the just.
(Luke 14:12–14)

Finally, it should not go unnoticed that while this petition in Matthew's formulation refers to debts and debtors, Jesus in his subsequent commentary uses other language: "trespasses" instead of "debts." There is a relationship between trespasses or sins and debts. That is more or less obvious in any system of jurisprudence and may possibly explain the Lucan version, which juxtaposes sins and the owing of indebtedness. Crimes committed against others require redress, compensation, restitution; and litigation is generally a means of acquiring it. If an anesthesiologist falls asleep during a surgery and the patient dies, the former is sued in order to gain adequate compensation.

Forgiveness As Opposed to the Spirit of Vengeance

What does forgiveness involve in such circumstances? The justice of the old covenant required "an eye for an eye, and a tooth for a tooth." The freedom of unobligedness and forgiveness are characteristic of God's new household. The incarnation of God's goodness and love have replaced the spirit of vengeance. As Jesus decreed in the fifth antithesis of the Sermon on the Mount:

You have heard that it was said, "An eye for an eye, and a tooth for a tooth." But I say to you, "Do not resist the wicked one! But whoever strikes you on the right cheek, turn to him [her] also the other. And to the one wanting to sue you and take your underwear, let him [her] also have your overgarment. And whoever presses you into service for one mile, go with him [her] two." (Matt. 5:38–41)

These three examples of responsive behavior over against the experience of the wickedness, sin, and transgression of others should not be interpreted as responses of submissive weakness. They are rather bold and creative actions that express the freedom and maturity out of which they arise, and they are directed at the termination of the vicious cycle of an eye for an eye and a tooth for a tooth. Some form of restitution may always be necessary, but it is not exacted as an expression of retaliation. The compensation that is claimed aspires to at-one-ment. Genuine forgiveness is the pursuit of goodness in love. It is unlimited, and it always involves an act of closure. The transgression, trespass, or sin that has been perpetrated is consigned to the oblivion of forgetfulness. Scars undoubtedly remain, but a new future is constituted in which the past and any of its memories that might persist hold no consequences for the continuing associations and relationships between human beings on all levels of their co-existence.

In conclusion it should not be overlooked that this petition for forgiveness does not stand at the beginning of the Lord's Prayer. Jesus assumes that repentance has already occurred. Reconciliation with God is an a priori reality for praying the prayer. Membership in God's household is not suspended until God is implored for absolution. While contriteness of heart and its verbalization in a plea for forgiveness are indispensable to the Lord's Prayer, the predominant consciousness in the Christian horizon of self-understanding that is presupposed for those who follow Jesus in praying his prayer is membership in God's new household as God's offspring of divinely human sons and daughters. Even before forgiveness is solicited, the activities in which God is engaged are affirmed by those who are praying the first three petitions and are actively collaborating with God in those same activities:

Your name be reverenced!

Your rule come!

Your will be done, as in heaven also on earth!

Moreover, the command of the fourth petition, the first directed to God ("Keep on giving us the bread that is necessary for our existence"), precedes the supplication for absolution. That means there could be no entreaty for daily bread if there were no ongoing family relationship between God and God's offspring. And God could not be directed to forgive if those praying this petition were not already engaged in the activity of forgiving others in the fulfillment of their identity as representatives of God's family. Praying for forgiveness implies the integrity of Christian identity in practicing forgiveness.

The identity of saint is prior to the identity of sinner for those who follow Jesus and pray his prayer. The latter, the identity of sinner, is never canceled during their earthly pilgrimage, but it is always the secondary and subordinate attribute of their Christian self-understanding.

Chapter 9

The Sixth and Seventh Petitions

"And do not bring us into being tested."

"But deliver us from the wicked one."

The Lord's Prayer is concluded with a set of petitions that, like the preceding two, employs the second person imperative. Once more God is being solicited with a twofold appeal. While the Lucan version ends abruptly with a negative formulation of its final entreaty, "do not bring," the Matthean parallel, which is also negative, is extended by a supplementary plea: "but deliver us from the wicked one." Although it is usually regarded as a separate, seventh petition, it serves primarily to complete and to clarify the previous petition to which it is attached by the conjunction "but."

In both versions this sixth petition, like the fifth before it, is introduced with the conjunction "and," indicating that the petition stands in some kind of continuity with the one that precedes it. In fact, the final three petitions of the Lord's Prayer, which address the founding Parent of this new household with a command, are joined by this conjunction. They express the critical needs of the members of this divine household insofar as they are involved in the stark realities of the old moral order: namely, the necessities of bread, forgiveness, and, in view of their participation in God's new moral order, the fearful and perilous consequences of incarnating the values of the kingdom of God.

This sixth petition is formulated with the negative particle *mê* ("not"), which requires the use of the subjunctive mood and is employed to express prohibition. In other words, "Prevent us from being tested!" or "Don't lead us into being tried!" That implies that God directs human beings into being tested and tried. But does God really do that sort of thing? Does God put the members of God's household to the test? And if so, why would God want to do that? What would God gain by doing that? Finally, what would the members of God's household profit from that?

Temptations as Tests

To answer these questions, it is necessary to clarify the word "temptation." The general associations of the word have been linked to the definitions that the dictionary offers: seduction, enticement, allurement, captivation. That is, temptations are seductions or enticements into activities animated by the lower nature of human beings. The apostle Paul refers to them as "the works of the flesh" and identifies among them "fornication, impurity, sensuality, idolatry, sorcery, enmity, strife, jealousy, fits of rage, selfishness, dissension, factions, envy, drunkenness, carousing, and things like these" (Gal. 5:19–21). Such behavior is often promoted by the cultural values of society and consequently contradicts the essential character of God's new household. Moreover, it subverts the witness to God's new moral order that the members of God's family are called to embody. Accordingly, such attitudes and activities may be considered to be temptations that endanger and undermine the kingdom or rule that God has entrusted into the hands of God's sons and daughters. This entreaty, therefore, is also a plea to be spared from becoming captivated by seductions of the lower nature or "the works of the flesh," which obscure and even efface Christian identity.

Second, it is essential to recognize that inducement into tests and trials is attributable to at least two different originators: human beings and God. Generally, perhaps, human beings believe that they motivate themselves, or at least are motivated by their lower nature, to submit to the enticements and obsessions that take possession of them, limit or even nullify their freedom, and destroy their humanity. There is the pursuit of self-indulgence and self-gratification. There is also the natural instinct of self-preservation and security, which expresses itself in defense mechanisms of various kinds to overcome anxiety and "to feel a basic sense of self-worth, of meaningfulness, of power."[1] Both arise out of the fear and denial of death and prevent human beings from entering more fully into the heritage of the new moral order: being truly free and "ruling in life" (Rom. 5:17). In Mark 14:38 Jesus warns his disciples, who had been sleeping while he was agonizing with God:

> Keep on watching and keep on praying so that you do not go into being tested.

The instinct for survival as well as the craving for quantity in life may engender behavior that is detrimental to a realization of a fuller and richer humanity as it is nurtured by participation in God's new moral order. Vigilance and prayer, however, according to Jesus' admonition, can thwart the temptations to establish security as well as the enticements to self-indulgence.

God is also to be identified as an instigator of temptations. Jesus' ministry, as narrated by the Gospels, offers frightening evidence of such divine initiatives. The most poignant instance is his struggle in the Garden of Gethsemane. Jesus is terrified by the test he is confronting and consequently prays:

> *Abba*, my Father, all things are possible to you. Remove this cup from me! But not what I want but what you [want].
> (Mark 14:36)

Will he endure the test that confronts him in his forthcoming passion? Will he retain his integrity? Will he remain faithful to *Abba* who generated him as *Abba's* Son, the new

---

1. Ernest Becker, *The Denial of Death* (New York: The Free Press, 1973), 59.

Human Being? And will he be able to maintain that identity throughout the ordeal that awaits him?

At this point it is necessary to make another critical differentiation. God may originate the temptation. God may lead Jesus and his disciples into temptation, but God does not do the actual testing. This is stated clearly in the Letter of James.

> Blessed is the human being who endures testing, because, being approved, he [she] will receive the crown of life which God promised to those who love him. Let no one who is being tested say, "I am being tested by God." For God is not tested by evil, and God tests no one. But each is tested by his [her] own desires being drawn away and enticed. Then desire conceiving breeds sin, and sin coming to maturity breeds death. (1:12–16)

This contradicts the perspective that is encountered in the Hebrew Scriptures. For example:

> After these things God tested Abraham and said to him, "Abraham!" And he said, "Here I am." He said, "Take your son, your only son Isaac, whom you love, and go to the land of Moriah, and offer him there as a burnt offering upon one of the mountains of which I shall tell you." (Gen. 22:1–2)

> Then Yahweh said to Moses, "Behold, I will rain bread from heaven for you; and the people shall go out and gather a day's portion every day, that I may test them, whether they will walk in my law or not." (Exod. 16:4)

> And Moses spoke to the people, "Do not fear, for God has come to test you, that the fear of him may be before your eyes, so that you may not sin." (Exod. 20:20)

> And you shall remember all the way which Yahweh your God has led you these forty years in the wilderness, that he might humble you, testing you to know what was in your heart, whether you would keep his commandments or not.
> (Deut. 8:2)

God, as the founding Parent of the household of Israel, does not hesitate to put his family to the test in order to have them demonstrate their obedience and thereby confirm their loyalty to the covenant that binds them together. That appears to be an early perspective in the history of Israel. The relationship within this household is hierarchical: God is the patriarch, and the people of Israel are his children; and this order of parent/child is maintained into the time of Jesus and beyond. But a significant reorientation begins to emerge in Wisdom tradition, specifically in the Book of Job, on the matter of testing.[2] Satan, who at this point is acknowledged to be one of God's sons, has become God's surrogate or agent as the tempter, and with God's permission he will put Job to the test in order to authenticate his loyalty.

In the new household of God horizontality has replaced verticality. God may be addressed as *Abba* but no longer within an order of patriarchy. As a result of Jesus' establishment of God's rule and his transference of that rule to his disciples, those who now participate in this divine household have come of age. They are no longer children but God's beloved adult daughters and sons. Accordingly, there is no longer any necessity for God to tempt or test their loyalty. They may be seduced by their own lower nature; they may be overcome by existential anxiety to develop defense mechanisms that will guarantee their security. But God will not tempt them in order to prove their faithfulness. Instead God's Spirit, who resides in each member of this reconstituted family, will serve as the Spirit of truth writing God's law on "the tablets of human hearts" and producing the fruits of "love, joy, peace, patience, kindness, goodness, faithfulness, gentleness, and self-control" (Gal. 5:22–23).

The Devil as the Tempter

It is Satan who has succeeded God as the tempter, but no longer in terms of the identity that the Book of Job ascribes

---

2. Compare 2 Samuel 24:1 with 1 Chronicles 21:1.

to him as one of God's sons. As the result of his transformation into the personification of evil, Satan has been identified with the devil, the transcendent power that rules the old moral order. In this capacity Satan, alias the devil, acts as the tempter, the one who tests God's sons and daughters.

Although God no longer tempts or tests those who belong to the new moral order, it is vital to recognize that God does lead Jesus into being tested and tried. That is evident in the story of Jesus' temptation in the wilderness.

> And immediately the Spirit cast him out into the wilderness; and he was in the wilderness forty days being tested by Satan. (Mark 1:12–13a)

> Then Jesus was led into the wilderness by the Spirit to be tested by the devil. (Matt. 4:1)

> Now Jesus, full of the Holy Spirit, returned from the Jordan, and he was led by the Spirit in the wilderness forty days being tested by the devil. (Luke 4:1–2)

In all three of the Synoptic Gospels the testing is done by the devil. But it is God's Spirit who leads Jesus into the wilderness in order to be tested. This crucial differentiation is confirmed by the supplementary appendage attached to this sixth petition in Matthew's version of the Lord's Prayer:

> And do not bring us into being tested, but deliver us from the wicked one.

Under the new moral order God tests no one. But God does lead Jesus into being tested by "the wicked one," the devil or Satan, in order to enter into conflict with the power of evil. That also appears to be the divine objective for Jesus' disciples.[3] Indeed, Jesus' call to discipleship is not only an entry into a new identity; it is also a summons to a new vocation. Identity presupposes vocation, the vocation of collaborating with God as God's adult sons and daughters in

---

3. Also E. Schweizer, *The Good News according to Matthew* (Atlanta: John Knox Press, 1975), 62.

the transformation of the world by abolishing all forms and forces of evil and thereby liberating the creation from its bondage to human corruption into the freedom and glory of God's offspring (Rom. 8:21).

Establishing the marks and boundaries of Christian identity tends to be as much of a Christian obsession today as Judaism's demarcation of Jewishness was during the time of Jesus. John the Baptizer excoriated his contemporaries for their preoccupation with identity to the exclusion of its inherent vocation.

> Generation of vipers! Who warned you to flee from the impending anger? Produce then fruit worthy of repentance! And do not begin to say to yourselves, "We have Abraham!" For I say to you, God is able to resurrect children to Abraham from these stones. (Matt. 3:7–9)

To entrust oneself to the security of Christian identity guarantees neither the present participation in God's rule nor a future with God in everlasting life. In the Sermon on the Mount (Matt. 7:21), Jesus states it bluntly: "Not everyone who says to me, 'Lord, Lord,' will enter into the kingdom of God, but the one who does the will of my Father in heaven." This reality is the experience of the five foolish virgins in the parable of the ten virgins. They are excluded from the wedding feast because they have not fulfilled their identity in the vocation of providing light for the bridegroom and his entourage as they proceed in the middle of the night to the home where the bride is waiting and where the marriage celebration will take place.

Christian vocation cannot be separated from Christian identity. Vocation expressed by concrete deeds and activities that promote justice and peace is the only valid sign of identity. Participation in God's rule necessarily includes conflict with evil. Jesus entered into his vocation immediately after his identity as God's beloved Son was established by the heavenly voice, and it involved him instantly in a conflict with evil. No account is given by Mark of the kinds of tests to which Satan subjected him. Matthew and Luke, however, recount three temptations.

The Three Testings of Jesus

The first is a test to act in continuity with the past in order to substantiate Jesus' new identity as God's Son: "If you are God's Son, speak so that these stones become loaves of bread" (Matt. 4:3). Since the plural (stones and loaves of bread) is employed by the devil, it would appear that this temptation involves more than self-gratification,[4] the satisfaction of his own hunger after fasting for forty days and nights. Such a marvelous production of bread would validate his baptismal presentation to Israel, at least in Matthew's Gospel, as the Messiah, the Son of God. Moses had brought forth water out of a rock (Num. 20:8). Jesus could establish his equality with Moses by transforming stones into loaves of bread. Such an imposing exploit would not only corroborate his new identity. It would also establish the continuity of Israelite typology; that is, Jesus as the fulfillment of Deuteronomy 18:15 and therefore the new Moses. Pattern is not only a vital source of meaning; it is also a seductive medium of security.

But Jesus refuses to establish himself as God's agent on the basis of Old Testament patterns and typologies. His call to repentance will not be authenticated by a personal resemblance to Israel's divinely appointed leaders and saviors. In accordance with God's self-identification to Moses, "I will be who I will be," God's activity in history does not move according to repetitive patterns of continuity. Jesus turns the temptation back to the devil with a quotation from Deu-

---

4. In Luke 4:4 the singular form of "stone" and "bread" is used instead of the plural. Perhaps the Lucan emphasis is on self-gratification. E. Schweizer in *The Good News according to Luke* (Atlanta: John Knox Press, 1984), 83, believes that the devil's challenge is "to still Jesus' hunger."

teronomy 8:3b, "The human being does not live by bread alone but by every word issuing from God's mouth." Even after a long period of fasting Jesus declines to satisfy his own hunger. As important as bread is for human survival, it is not enough to sustain human life.

Under the same words Jesus also repudiates that understanding of human existence that is determined by the priority of material security: not only the fulfillment of physical needs but also equally the security of sameness instead of difference, likeness instead of contrast, conformity instead of diversity. In the subsequent course of his ministry he will multiply bread and fish in order to satisfy the hunger of the impoverished crowds, but only at the end of the day after he has taught them about the kingdom of God and healed them.

The second temptation is a challenge to prove his identity as God's Son to his contemporaries on the basis of an ultimate accumulation of holiness: God's Word, God's temple on God's mount in God's city of Jerusalem.

> If you are God's Son, throw yourself down. For it is written: "To his angels he will give orders concerning you, and on hands they will lift you lest you strike your foot against a stone." (Matt. 4:6)

If the human being lives by every word issuing from God's mouth, according to Jesus' quotation of Deuteronomy 8:3b, then Jesus should be able to trust God's Word, above all at the center of the world, the temple in Jerusalem, where God's name dwells. What a dazzling effect that would have on the religious sensitivities of his fellow Jews: to be divinely authenticated before them by an unprecedented exploit! In contrast to the first temptation, there is no pattern of continuity, no biblical typology conveyed by a death-defying leap from the highest point of the temple. No king, high priest, or prophet in Old Testament history had ever attempted such a feat.

If identity is expressed through vocation and both arise out of God's call to partnership for the specific purpose of transforming the world, then both identity and vocation can be authenticated by proving God's Word to be true through an awe-inspiring jump from the parapet of the temple. Such a religious act at the architectonic center of the world would not only certify Jesus and guarantee an immense response among his contemporaries to discipleship; for Jesus himself it would confirm God's trustworthiness.

This second test turns out to be a double temptation. Jesus is being tested, but he is also being challenged to test God's reliability. The latter is a critical issue. If God leads God's own sons and daughters into conflict with evil, God's dependability and trustworthiness are vital concerns. Will God uphold the divine promises? Will God be faithful to God's own Word?

Jesus, however, not only rejects the temptation to test God but also repudiates the inducement to captivate followers for the kingdom of God on the basis of religious showmanship and miraculous spectacle. The new moral order of God's rule brings with it its own inducements. Jesus responds to the devil's twofold challenge with another quotation from Moses' last will and testament in the Book of Deuteronomy. He meets Scripture with Scripture.

> Again it is written, you shall not put the Lord your God to the test. (6:17)

God's faithfulness is not a measurable quantity. It is not to be tested or proven to confirm identity or vocation for the sake of personal security. At the same time, the reality of the new moral order and its attendant integrity of identity and vocation are not to be established by an elite display of power and authority.

In the third test Jesus is offered a glimpse of the objective of his vocation: "all the kingdoms of the world and their glory." At the beginning of Israel's history Moses had viewed from Mount Nebo "all the land" that Israel would have to subdue in order to fulfill God's will. In contrast, Jesus, from a high mountain, is confronted with the universal mission of uniting the world under the rule of God, which he has been called to constitute. After rejecting the use of miraculous spectacle and the elitist power and authority that it would display, Jesus is confronted with a seemingly irresistible offer:

> All these things I will give you, if falling down you will worship me. (Matt. 4:9)

No longer is he being challenged to validate his identity as God's Son. Jesus has effectively demonstrated the inner strength of his self-understanding without resorting to any overt forms of self-authentication. This, however, is the ultimate temptation: to achieve God's objective by the simple act of worshiping the devil, to fulfill God's will by subordinating oneself to the power of evil, to unite the power structures of the world under one dominating rule in order to eliminate poverty and injustice. Such an apparent bargain has seduced many ideologically controlled, would-be messiahs down through the centuries. For does not the end justify the means?

But, as Jesus recognizes, worshiping the devil results in the loss of the freedom and autonomy that God wills for all human beings. Any and every submission to the powers of darkness perpetuates the diabolical cycle of exchanging one form of oppression for another. For lordship in any form, whether over a single ethnic community or all of humanity, as history has repeatedly manifested, is only a continuation of the hierarchical structures that promote oppression, exploitation, and dispossession.

Jesus drives away the devil with another text from Deuteronomy:

> Go away, Satan! For it is written, "The Lord your God you shall worship, and him alone you shall serve! (Matt. 4:10)

Jesus refuses to surrender his divinely appointed sovereignty to the devil. In his freedom as God's beloved Son he will worship and serve God by fulfilling God's will, and that will involve him in a divine egalitarian partnership in the actualization of God's rule. Eventually, at his resurrection from the dead, he will acknowledge the acquisition of what Satan had offered him in this third temptation:

> All authority in heaven and on earth was given to me.
>
> (Matt. 28:18)

But he will have received it from God on the basis of his worship and service in fulfilling God's will and actualizing God's rule.

The Prospect of Being Tested

God does lead God's daughters and sons into conflict with evil, and it is a terrifying prospect. Jesus' prayer in the Garden of Gethsemane expresses his dread of what he anticipates in his imminent crucifixion. The extreme prejudice originating from the guardians of society who want to maintain the status quo and the rich and the powerful who have the most to lose in the transformation of the world may result in death, torture, imprisonment, banning (as in South Africa during the era of apartheid), excommunication, ostracism, hostility, rejection. The consequences will vary according to time and place and socioeconomic and political context, but whatever they may be, they will inflict pain and suffering. *Foxe's Book of Martyrs* recounts the stories of many individuals who in the course of the first eighteen hundred years of the Christian movement suffered death, torture, and banishment because of their Christian witness.[5] The same consequences continue to be experienced by countless human beings who have entered into conflict with evil in order to reconstitute society for a greater actualization of justice and peace. Many of them, such as Dietrich Bonhoeffer,

---

5. See also W. H. C. Frend, *Martyrdom and Persecution in the Early Church* (Garden City, N.Y.: Doubleday, 1967).

Martin Luther King, Jr., Beyers Naudé, and Nelson Mandela, are revered and serve as models of the kind of Christian witness that are needed.

It is appropriate, therefore, that this entreaty concludes the Lord's Prayer. As the third petition that is addressed to God by the use of the second person imperative, it follows naturally from the preceding two petitions to which it is linked. Initially the members of God's household have expressed their support of God's activities in the world, activities in which they themselves are engaged: reverencing God's name, extending God's rule, and fulfilling God's will. In these final petitions they appeal to God for bread necessary for existence, for forgiveness of debts and sins and their continuation of the freedom of God's household from obligation, and finally for deliverance from the horror of conflict with evil. These especially are the critical realities of their daily lives as they fulfill their identity as God's sons and daughters in their vocational activity of incarnating and actualizing God's rule.

In view of this vocational activity to fulfill Christian identity, there is always the threat of being put to the test by a confrontation with the powers of darkness. The link between the petition "Your kingdom come!" and the petition "Do not lead us into being tested, but deliver us from the wicked one" is true to life. Therefore, given the grim consequences that may result from participation in God's rule, Jesus ends this prayer with a plea to be delivered from the dread consequences of engagement with evil: "Do not lead us into being tested, but deliver us from the wicked one."

Chapter 10

The Doxology

*"For yours is the kingdom and the power
and the glory forever."*

"Amen."

Traditionally the Lord's Prayer has been concluded with a doxology that acknowledges what God is due as God from those who embrace their membership in God's family but who at the same time acknowledge their creaturehood. However, neither the Lucan nor the Matthean formulation of the prayer ends with this doxology. It appears for the first time in the church's earliest catechism, the *Didache*, but without the word "kingdom":

> For yours is the power and the glory forever.

None of the three versions concludes with an Amen. That may have been presupposed, for the liturgy of the early church that is reflected in the writings of the New Testament evidently voiced the Amen recurrently, especially following the intonation of doxologies.[1] Eventually the Amen, like the doxology that precedes it, was incorporated into the manuscript tradition of Matthew's formulation of the Lord's Prayer, probably because it became the preferred version of the prayer in the developing liturgy of the church.

The difference between the wording of the concluding doxology in the *Didache* and the wording that has become

---

1. See Romans 1:25; 9:5, 11:30; Galatians 1:5; Ephesians 3:21; Philippians 4:20; 1 Timothy 1:17; 6:16; 2 Timothy 4:18; Hebrews 13:21; 1 Peter 4:11; 5:11; Jude 25; Revelation 1:6.

106

dominant in the subsequent tradition into the present-day form is more significant. It is the word "kingdom." Why is "kingdom" absent in the earliest construct of the doxology in the *Didache?* When, why, and in what context was it incorporated?

God's Rule Belongs to God's Adult Daughters and Sons

In view of the witness that various New Testament texts specify about this eschatological reality, the kingdom or the kingdom of God, the inclusion of the word "kingdom" in the doxology must be regarded as a mistake. It should never have been added to the formulation of the doxology that appears in the *Didache* for the simple reason that the kingdom of God is the legacy of the church. It was entrusted by Jesus to his disciples. It belongs to them! It is the birthright of God's family of daughters and sons and therefore is to be exercised by everyone who identifies with this household. That is already anticipated in the apocalyptic prophecy of Daniel. God delivers God's rule to the saints. God inaugurated that rule, that kingdom, as Daniel 2:44–45 indicates, but subsequently hands it over to "the people of the saints of the Most High." They will exercise it on God's behalf.

> And the kingdom and the dominion and the greatness of the kingdoms under the whole heaven shall be given to the people of the saints of the Most High. Their kingdom shall be an everlasting kingdom, and all dominions shall serve and obey them. (Dan. 7:27)

All four Gospels present Jesus acting as God's agent and surrogate to fulfill his vocational call to actualize this apocalyptic vision of God's new moral order. But it is not a kingdom in which he alone is the sovereign king who rules on behalf of God. It is rather a kingdom whose rule and sovereignty he shares with his followers. Jesus in Luke 12:32 exhorts his disciples:

> Stop fearing, little flock! For your Father is pleased to give you the kingdom.

Eventually, at the institution of the Eucharist in the context of the Passover, he assigns the kingdom to them:

> You are the ones who have continued with me in my testings; and I ordain for you as my Father ordained for me a kingdom. (Luke 22:28–29)

The Acts of the Apostles, volume 2 of Luke's literary work, narrates the story of the disciples beginning to take responsibility for this gift, incarnating it, as Jesus did, and bringing it into being throughout the Greco-Roman world.

Jesus' incorporation of his disciples in the rule of God which he has inaugurated is also expressly transmitted in Matthew's Gospel. In 16:19 Peter, who became the ideal disciple and therefore also the representative of God's new people by joining Jesus in walking on the sea and manifesting lordship over chaos, is awarded the keys to God's rule.

> I will give you the keys of the kingdom of the heavens, and whatever you bind on earth will be bound in heaven, and whatever you loose on earth will be loosed in the heavens.

The power of the keys is not to determine the destiny of other human beings by locking or unlocking the gates of God's kingdom. The gender of the relative pronoun is neuter. Peter is given the authority to build the world of God's new moral order: to establish as well as to dissolve systemic structures, institutions, and programs, and to constitute ethical conduct and community practice. But always and only on the basis of the distinctive character of God's rule: justice, equality, and inclusiveness!

Additionally, the extraordinary conclusion of Matthew's Gospel deserves to be recalled in this context. In this culminating episode the eleven of the twelve who had been appointed by Jesus to constitute the new people of God journey to the predesignated mountain in Galilee in order to encounter the risen Jesus. After he claims "all authority in heaven and on earth," he commissions them to make disciples of the whole world. Nothing is explicitly reported about their empowerment for the fulfillment of this vocation, as, for example, in Acts 2:1–4. But it is intimated in the closing pledge Jesus makes to his disciples:

> See, I with you am even to the consummation of the age.
>
> (Matt. 28:20)

Eleven had ascended into the mountain. Twelve descend. Jesus has entered the incomplete circle of the eleven as the twelfth in order to accompany them into the world to fulfill God's will. As the twelfth he not only reconstitutes the new people of God; as a member of this community he also establishes a horizontal relationship within this family by sharing with his brothers and sisters his identity as the new Human Being as well as "all authority in heaven and on earth," which he has received from God. On this final architectonic center, which is immediately left behind, the community of the new humanity is born, and in fulfillment of the Great Commission, its members journey with him into the world in order to draw others into God's rule in which they themselves now participate.

Jesus' closing words draw his followers into his identity as Emmanuel, "God with us" (Matt. 1:23). He is "I am." And his followers, by being enclosed in his "I with you am," share in his deification and its empowerment as fellow sons and daughters of God.

In 1 Corinthians 15:24–28 the apostle Paul also bears witness to the allocation of the kingdom to the care and accountability of the church as the body of Christ.

> Then the end, when he [the Christ] will deliver up the kingdom to God and Father, when he has abolished every rule and every authority and power. For it is necessary that he

rules until he puts all the enemies under his feet. The last
enemy that is to be abolished is death. For he subjected all
things under his feet. But when it says that all things have
been subjected, it is clear that the one who subjected all
things to him is excepted. Now when all things have been
subjected to him, the Son will be subjected to the One who
subjected all things to him, so that God is all things in all
things.

For Paul Christ is the new creation of the One and the Many.
Concretely it is the reality of the body of Christ, both Jesus
the resurrected, glorified, and enthroned Lord and all those
who in their historical existence participate in his transcendence. In other words, it is Jesus and all who incarnate the
new moral order in their everyday life. As the apostle asserts
in 1 Corinthians 12:12:

> For even as the body is one and has many members, but all
> the members of the body being many are one body, so also
> the Christ.

Consequently the focus of his eschatology is not merely the
individual Jesus who is the Christ. It is this corporate reality
of the church as the body of Christ. The new humanity Jesus
constituted is the community of the One and the Many, in
which there is no place for any dualism of the clean and the
unclean.

It is the body of Christ, therefore, the One and the Many,
that has been entrusted with the continued actualization and
exercise of God's rule. This care and accountability will belong to the church as the body of Christ, in collaboration
with the resurrected, glorified, and enthroned Jesus Christ,
until all the powers and principalities have been abolished,
until all the forms and forces of death have been eradicated
from human existence.[2] That may require a very lengthy period of time, perhaps thousands of years. Only when this
assignment has been completed, when the body of Christ has

---

2. See Walter Wink, *Engaging the Powers: Discernment and Resistance in a
World of Domination* (Minneapolis: Fortress, 1992), especially chaps. 3–8.

brought about God's rule in all of its fullness and universality — in partnership with God! — only then will the old
moral order come to an end. And at that moment in time
and history the parousia of the new Human Being, or the so-
called second coming, will take place in order to culminate
the union of the transcendent resurrected and glorified Jesus
and the historical reality of his body, the Christ, and to return the kingdom to God. At that ultimate realization of the
divine objective, "God will be all things in all things."

The kingdom still belongs to God's household. It is the
legacy of those who participate in the new moral order and
incarnate its realities in their lives. Some day it will be returned to God. But in the meantime, as its absence in the
doxology of the *Didache* indicates, it does not belong to the
conclusion of the Lord's Prayer.

The version of the Lord's Prayer in the *Didache*, which is
almost identical to that in Matthew 6:9–13, indicates that
the Matthean formulation of the prayer was beginning to
become widely adopted in the worship life of the church.
Most likely it was in this context of liturgical usage that
the doxology was appended to the prayer. Its addition may
have been a natural development fostered by liturgical tradition. Or, early Christians may have been motivated to
conclude the Lord's Prayer with a doxology in order to coun-
teract the contemporaneous political ideology of the emperor
cult. Such an incentive is supported by the politically con-
ditioned prayers and hymns preserved in the Revelation to
John, which attribute glory, honor, and power to God over
against the claims made by the self-deifying emperors of the
Roman Empire.

When the word "kingdom" was incorporated into the
doxology is probably indeterminable. Its inclusion occurred
liturgically in the worship life of the ancient church well before the doxology itself was interpolated into the text of the
Lord's Prayer in Matthew 6:13. The earliest witness to this
textual expansion appears to be the fifth-century Washington

Codex (housed in the Smithsonian Institution in Washington, D.C.). Many other manuscripts and manuscript families, however, testify to its wide circulation throughout the ancient church: the eighth-century Codex Regius (L or 019), the ninth-century Koridethi (038), the eighth-century uncial 0233, the minuscule family of F12 spanning the tenth through the fifteenth centuries, the majority of the minuscule codices, the early Latin readings preserved in the church fathers, and finally the Syriac and the Coptic Sahidic and Bohairic translations.

Ultimately the kingdom is to be attributed to God as much as are power and glory. God is their originator, and all human beings in an acknowledgment of their creaturehood rightfully ascribe them to God. But creaturehood is divinely endowed with both power and glory, as Psalm 8 affirms in its celebration of God's creation of the human being in God's own image and likeness.

> When I look at your heavens, the work of your fingers, the moon and the stars which you have established, what is the human being that you are mindful of him [her], and the son of the human being that you care for him [her]? You have made them little less than God and crowned them with glory and honor. You have given them dominion over the works of your hands. You have put all things under their feet. (8:3–6)

On the basis of the first creation, humanity consists of human beings who, although they are made in the image and likeness of God and therefore are crowned with glory and honor, are constituted as living souls or living selves. This humanity, however, has become infected with the disease of sin and is subject to and victimized by the forms and forces of death that dominate the old moral order. In contrast, human beings who participate in the new creation that God established by raising Jesus Christ from the dead belong to a new humanity that consists of life-giving spirits.

> So it is written: "the first Adam became a living soul, the last Adam a life-giving spirit." (1 Cor. 15:45)

Transformation and Empowerment

This new humanity, pioneered by Jesus of Nazareth, participates in God's power by the indwelling of God's Spirit. By this empowerment God's adult daughters and sons are enabled to exercise God's rule in their lives and simultaneously extend God's rule in the world. In fulfilling their identity by involvement in their vocation they are also undergoing a metamorphosis, the kind that Jesus disclosed in his transfiguration. To quote the apostle Paul again:

> Now we all, with unveiled face, contemplating the glory of the Lord, are being metamorphosed into the same image from glory into glory, even as it is from the Lord of the Spirit.
> (2 Cor. 3:18)

Metamorphosis or transformation into the image and likeness of the new Adam is the destiny of all who are members of God's household. It is a gradual, unfolding change that results in greater and greater freedom

> from the spirit of vengeance
> from the fear of death
> from the infection of sin and the alienation it generates.

It is a process of transcending the nature of the old Adam by being converted into a divinely human being, as divinely human as Jesus is disclosed to have been in the Gospels of the New Testament. It is a process of being healed of brokenness and estrangement. It is a process of realizing the glory of God by becoming more free and fully alive in the chaos, uncertainty, and contingency of daily life. It is a process that eventuates in everlasting life and culminates in being drawn into the life and being of God.

Ultimately kingdom, power, and glory are attributable to God and to God alone. But kingdom throughout the age of the new moral order belongs to the members of God's new household until they, in collaboration with God, have lib-

erated the creation from its bondage to corruption into the
glory into which they have been transformed (Rom. 8:21).
Power, which originates from God, is shared by God with all
of humanity in countless forms, but especially with those in
whom God's Spirit resides in order to fulfill God's will. And
glory, the glory of God, is the destiny that God wills for all
human beings, not exclusively for those who gain political
and economic power in a nation-state. God wills it for all
human beings in historical existence and beyond in the life
that is to come.

Amen

The only purposeful response to all of these petitions and to
the doxology by those who belong to God's household is the
ancient *amen*. It is a Hebrew word derived from the verb
'mn, which bears a variety of meanings in its different verbal
forms: be faithful, established, stand firm, believe.

> Within the Hebrew Bible, "Amen" typically appears at
> the close of commands, blessings, curses, doxologies, and
> prayers. Fundamentally, it is used to confirm what has been
> said before, by way of response.[3]

Genoito, or "so be it," is the preferred rendering of the Hebrew *amen* in the Septuagint.[4] In a few instances, namely,
1 Chronicles 16:36 and Nehemiah 5:13 and 8:6, the Hebrew
is transliterated into Greek as *amên*. Two apocryphal books
of the Old Testament, 1 Esdras 9:47 and Tobit 8:8 and
14:15, indicate that its usage as an affirmative response to
prayers of blessing and intercession was beginning to extend
into the Greek-speaking world.[5]

---

3. Bruce Chilton, "Amen," in *The Anchor Bible Dictionary*, ed. David Noel
Freedman (New York: Doubleday, 1992), 1:185.
4. Ibid.
5. Ibid.

When he opened the law, they all stood erect. And Ezra blessed the Lord God Most High, the God of hosts, the Almighty, and the multitude answered, "Amen."

(1 Esd. 9:46–47)

In Tobit 8:5 Sarah joins Tobias in prayer before they consummate their marriage:

Blessed are you, O God of our ancestors, and blessed is your name in all generations forever. Let the heavens and the whole creation bless you forever. You made Adam, and for him you made his wife Eve as a helper and support. From the two of them the human race has sprung. You said, "It is not good that the man should be alone; let us make a helper for him like himself." I now am taking this kinswoman of mine, not because of lust but with sincerity. Grant that she and I may find mercy and that we may grow old together.

(Tob. 8:5–7)

And they both said, "Amen, Amen." (Tob. 8:8)

English translations of the Hebrew Scriptures also transliterate the Hebrew *amen* into Amen, as in Numbers 5:22, Deuteronomy 27:15–26, 1 Kings 1:36, Jeremiah 28:6, Psalm 41:13, Nehemiah 5:13, and 1 Chronicles 16:36.[6] All of these are responses of affirmation to pronouncements, curses, and blessings. The *amen* in Jeremiah 11:5 bears the same sense of affirmation but is usually rendered "So be it!"

In the New Testament the letters of the apostle Paul attest to its currency in the life and liturgy of the early church. The examples that have already been cited indicate that his employment of the Amen is traditional and follows its conventional use as a responsive affirmation. Nevertheless, as an utterance of affirmation it cannot but be affected by his self-understanding of being a member of God's new household of adult sons and daughters, empowered by the Holy Spirit and involved in a process of being transformed into the image and likeness of the new Human Being from one degree of glory into another. Accordingly, for Paul Amen is a

---

6. See also Psalm 72:19; 89:52; 106:48.

resounding "So be it!" It is a response that is weighted with confidence, conviction, and certainty. Joined to the Lord's Prayer, therefore, it is a reinforcement of all its petitions as well as its doxology. And when it is spoken in faith with the self-consciousness of being God's beloved daughters and sons, it is an affirmation that *Abba* God is committed to the fulfillment of all the petitions of the prayer. For the petitions of the Lord's Prayer are quintessentially the expressions of God's will and objective for all human beings and for the world in which they live, move, and have their being.

Epilogue

Personal engagement with the Creator of the universe engenders an awesome relationship of mutuality. The willingness to risk talking to God, while at the same time being self-critical of the motivation and objectives of the prayers we speak, results in a prodigious enrichment of our humanity. Since we may not always know what is fitting for us to pray, a model is useful, if not indispensable. And what better model than the Lord's Prayer? It is comprehensive, and, according to the Gospels of Matthew and Luke, Jesus himself formulated it.

But the Lord's Prayer has become a frozen or hardened tradition. Only one version, that of Matthew 6:9–13, is generally prayed throughout the Christian world, at least in the major denominations of Protestantism and in the Roman Catholic Church. At the beginning of the Christian movement, however, this tradition was more dynamic, open to change and adaptation. In our time it seems that only a few Christian communities, mostly ethnic, show no fear or hesitation in adapting the Lord's Prayer to the language and thought forms of their own culture. An excellent example is a Maori formulation of the Lord's Prayer.

> Eternal Spirit!
> Earthmaker, Painbearer, Lifegiver,
> Source of all that is and that shall be,
> Father and Mother of us all,
> Loving God, in whom is heaven:
> The hallowing of your name echo through the universe!
> The way of your justice be followed by the peoples of the
> earth!
> Your heavenly will be done by all created beings!

Your commonwealth of peace and freedom sustain our hope
    and come in earth.
With the bread we need for today, feed us.
In the hurts we absorb from one another, forgive us.
In times of temptation and test, strengthen us.
From trials too great to endure, spare us.
From the grip of all that is evil, free us.
For you reign in the glory of the power that is love, now and
    forever. Amen.[1]

Because the Matthean formulation of the Lord's Prayer continues to be prayed without many linguistic or cultural
adaptations, the prayer has become virtually meaningless
and consequently is prayed by rote in services of worship.

Hardened tradition is lifeless and empty. Unless reformulations of the Lord's Prayer are undertaken, reformulations
that include its adaptation to our cultural context and the
renovation of its antiquated language, the prayer will continue to be meaningless in public worship and abandoned in
private devotion.

The Gospels of the New Testament set a precedent for
undertaking revisions of the Lord's Prayer. The Christian
community of the Gospel according to Matthew did not hesitate to adapt the shorter version of the prayer preserved
in Luke 11:2–4 by enlarging it in ways that expressed its
distinctive theological and spiritual perspective. Should not
this unreserved openness to meaningful change be recovered,
especially for a more dynamic entry into the twenty-first century? Little changes, of course, are being made here and
there. Words like "debts" and "debtors" as well as "trespasses" are being replaced by "sins" and "sin." But more
than that is needed to revitalize the Lord's Prayer for its use
in public worship and private devotion.

As the preface acknowledges, there are two kinds of
prayers: spontaneous cries from the heart and the more

---

1. From the New Zealand Maori Anglican Liturgy. Thanks to Woodley and
Julie White!

formal liturgical prayers that are spoken in worship. Spontaneous, unpremeditated prayers belong to the fundamental condition of being in life and being in the world. They will be voiced as long as human beings continue to exist.

Formal prayers have their own legitimacy in corporate worship and community life. The only formal prayer that lay worshipers generally know is the Lord's Prayer, and it is probably little understood. Yet as a formal prayer its content is complete. Its petitions include those realities of the world in which God is involved and those realities of life that concern human beings. This is as true of the briefer Lucan version of the prayer as it is of the expanded formulation in Matthew's Gospel.

It is time, therefore, to begin to rehabilitate the Lord's Prayer, to amend its language and to make its content more transparent to those who are praying it. Any revision that is undertaken, however, should correspond to the intent of the prayer's individual petitions. Attendantly indispensable as a frame of reference for the praying of the Lord's Prayer is that distinctive Christian self-understanding of being an adult member of God's household, an adult who "is seated with Christ in the heavenly places" (Eph. 2:6) and therefore co-enthroned with God.

Living in that horizon of consciousness nurtures within me a sense of response-ability to fulfill my identity as a Christian to collaborate with God in continuing the work that Jesus inaugurated, promoting and expanding God's rule on earth. God's rule, however, belongs to God only ultimately and finally (1 Cor. 15:24–28). In the present it is the legacy we have inherited from and through Jesus Christ. To exercise God's rule in our lives, therefore, involves us in the kinds of activities Jesus engaged in throughout his ministry:

> the pursuit of justice and peace;
> the termination of all forms of retaliation;
> the transmission of health and wholeness in the world which
>   we inhabit;

embodying the love of 1 Corinthians 13;

being open, vulnerable and inclusive in our relationships to
  others;

living and acting out the empowerment of God's indwelling
  Spirit;

contributing as liberally as we can to the needs of all our
  fellow human beings;

accepting and fulfilling our servanthood in the freedom and
  sovereignty we have as members of God's household.

This is the horizon of consciousness from within which
I believe the Lord's Prayer is to be prayed. It is the self-
understanding I am called to embrace as a disciple of Jesus
Christ. Yet after stating this, I must quickly add the acknowledgment I have appropriated from the apostle Paul to
account for my own failures in fulfilling this response-ability:

> so that I might know him and the power of his resurrection
> and the fellowship of his sufferings, becoming like him in his
> death, if somehow I might attain to the resurrection of the
> dead. Not that I already obtained [it] or that I already have
> been perfected, but I am pursuing [it] to make it my own,
> because Christ Jesus has made me his own. (Phil. 3:10–12)

If the Lord's Prayer is to have any meaning for me, I must
pray it responsibly. I can do that, I am convinced, only if I
embrace my identity as an adult member of God's household,
while at the same time I continue to live in the world and
relate to others in the vulnerability of a child.

> Unless you turn and become as children, you will by no
> means enter into the kingdom of the heavens. (Matt. 18:3)

As I strive to live as an adult of God with a childlike openness to the world, I engage in the work to which I have been
called: to serve as God's mouthpiece, hands, and feet. I pray
the Lord's Prayer as a member of God's family, speaking to
God as my Parent and using a form of address that conveys the intimacy of our relationship. Jesus preferred *Abba*
(Papa), but for me it has to be a term or a title that expresses

the warmth and closeness of family mutuality, sometimes Papa, sometimes Mama, or sometimes a little more formally as Father or Mother. But there are other possibilities.

As soon as I have expressed this cherished familiarity, I proceed to affirm the holiness of my heavenly Parent's name. Since the name, however, also represents the person, I am attesting to the holiness of God's being and voicing the disposition I share with the other members of this divine household that God be held in awe and worshiped by all of us who are praying the Lord's Prayer and ultimately by all the peoples of the earth.

I pray the second petition, "Your rule come!" in the same way as the first. That is, I join in expressing the will of God's household — which corresponds to the will of God — that all human beings be drawn into God's reign as quickly as possible for their sakes and for the sake of the whole creation. Since God's rule is already here and now and I am participating in it, I do not entreat God to bring about that reality. Like God and like all the members of God's family, I want all my fellow human beings to belong to God's household and to experience the great benefits of God's rule in their lives. In this way I unite with God and God's family in summoning its final actualization, and with it the fulfillment of God's will.

In and through these petitions I have voiced the initiatives God is pursuing in the world. But I have spoken them as a member of God's household who, with my sisters and brothers, is actively engaged in contributing to the realization of those initiatives. In the remaining petitions I verbalize both my needs and the needs of those with whom I am praying, and these I address directly to God by the use of the second person imperative.

"Keep on giving us the bread we need for our existence." Acquiring daily bread is no problem for me, but it may be for others; and therefore I want to be in solidarity with them. "Bread" signifies more than food. It represents all the things that are essential to our flesh-and-blood existence:

clothing, shelter, work, sustenance, and not the least, nour-
ishment for our psychic mode of being and our growth into
the spirituality of the body of Christ.

Both versions of the fifth petition have great meaning for
me. Because I grew up in a family where the obligation of
reciprocity determined our relationship with others, I have
found Matthew's formulation especially significant. I need to
be reminded continuously that God has set me free from all
obligation, even in my relationship to my heavenly Parent.
Yet I must also be prompted to remember that reciprocity is
not the basis of my association with my fellow human beings. They are not obliged to me, no matter how much I
do for them, even as I am not obliged to them, no matter
how much they do for me. To substitute the word "sin" in
place of "debts" is also meaningful, because I hurt and injure
others with my thoughtless words and deeds, my loveless-
ness, my self-centered actions, my lack of care and concern.
Consequently, I need and I want forgiveness for both the
debts that I incur in my relationship with God and the sins
that I commit in my relationship with others.

Finally, I know that my heavenly Parent needs my mouth,
my hands, and my feet in order to consummate the divine
plan for the liberation of all human beings and their transformation into the image of Jesus Christ, the first final Human
Being. I want to serve as God's agent for justice and peace
in the world, and I know that my identity as God's offspring
is fulfilled in the performance of the work to which I believe I have been called. Discharging those response-abilities
may engender conflict, arouse hostility, and result in rejection. But generally such incidents and circumstances are not
life-threatening ordeals. What I fear, what arouses anxiety
and even dread in me, is the possibility of God conducting
me into a confrontation with the power of evil, or, as this
petition expresses it, putting me to the test.

The Gospels make it clear that God does not do the
testing. That is carried out by evil as it embodies itself in in-

stitutions and the human beings who deify those institutions and give their allegiance to them. God, however, requires human voices, human hands and feet, to subvert the powers of darkness and terminate the evil that continues to crush human life. It is possible, therefore, that I may be led or drawn into a conflict with transcendent evil, the systemic evil of institutions. In view of the weaknesses of my mortality, I may not prevail in maintaining my integrity as an adult member of God's household. Like Peter, I may end up denying Jesus with a curse of renunciation. Or like Judas, I may even surrender myself to the power of evil and end up collaborating with it. The sobering recognition of my own frailty compels me to pray that I be delivered from that kind of a test. More moderate activities, which usually are not life-threatening, such as bearing witness to God's will for justice and peace, uniting with others in the struggle against racism, sexism, economic exploitation, and political oppression, are generally endurable in the fulfillment of my response-abilities as a member of God's household. I have no difficulty in involving myself in them, although I may often fail in discharging them.

Now that I have reached the conclusion of the Lord's Prayer, having expressed my support for God's activities in the world as a member of God's family involved in those same activities and having voiced the needs that I share with other members of God's family, I end with an acknowledgment that intimates my profound gratitude. The gifts that God shares with me, kingdom, power, and glory, ultimately and finally belong to God. With that affirmation the yearning that is reinforced deep within me is the advent of that consummation when "God will be all things in all things."

In the light of all that has been said, how would I go about revising the Lord's Prayer in order to make its content more intelligible to Christians today? How would I adapt it to the realities of our own society and its culture, employing language that reveals rather than conceals? Many revisions are possible, and those who reach this closure of the book may want to improvise a version of their own. The reformulation I offer expresses the comprehension I have gained of the Lord's Prayer through this study.

> Indwelling and ever present God!
> Our Heavenly Mother who has given birth to us!
> Our Heavenly Father who calls us into mutual activity!
> We hold you in awe and summon all to join us in honoring
>   you.
> We gratefully participate in your reign as we support its
>   expansion throughout the world.
> We affirm your will for justice and peace as we continue to
>   work for their realization.
> But keep on supporting us with the food we need for body
>   and soul.
> Forgive our sins and our indebtedness, as we forgive them to
>   others.
> Enable us to recognize evil and avoid its influence.
> Empower us for your service, but spare us from trials too
>   great to endure.
> For to you belong all sovereignty, power, and glory, finally
>   and forever,
> and we praise and worship you for sharing them with us.
>   Amen.

Glossary

Apocalypse: a Greek word meaning "unveiled" or "revealed"; a designation given to a class of writings that disclose future events, like the last book of the Bible, the Revelation to John.

Apocalypticism: a perspective or ideology that is millennial; that is, an attitude that looks to the future for divine judgment on the present moral order and the inauguration of a new creation, a new moral order.

Architectonic center: usually a sacred city that is related to a sacred mountain that may have a temple built on it in which a god is believed to dwell. A navel or axis mundi, often a capital city, like Jerusalem.

Aorist: the past tense in Greek that has the character of being an indefinite point in past time.

Benedictus: a Latin word meaning "blessed" that serves as the designation of the song that Simeon sang when he encountered Jesus in the temple of Jerusalem. See Luke 2:25–35.

Christology, christological: a teaching or doctrine of a messianic figure, like Jesus Christ, to whom titles are ascribed ("Son of God," "Son of Man," "Lord") that express specific aspects of activity that are aimed at the renewal of society and those who participate in it.

Day of Atonement or Yom Kippur: a Jewish high holy day celebrated on the tenth day of the month of Tishri, the first month of the Jewish civil calendar, which involves fasting, repentance, the forgiveness of sins, and reconciliation with God.

Didache: the earliest Christian catechism or book of teaching on the Christian faith, its sacraments, and its ethical way of life, dated at the end of the first or the beginning of the second century of the common era (A.D.)

Eponymous: naming a clan or tribe after its founder, for example, Abraham or Jacob.

Eschatology, eschatological: a teaching or doctrine that anticipates a goal or end of history, which determines how life is to be lived in the present. Certain books of the New Testament convey the actualization of the long-awaited arrival of a new creation or a new humanity through the death and resurrection of Jesus. Because resurrection is a corporate event, a span of time is necessary after Jesus' resurrection to make possible the resurrection of those who follow him in discipleship. When that process has been completed, the parousia or second coming will take place.

Gentile: a non-Jew, a person of non-Jewish ancestry.

Intertestamental: that period of time between the Hebrew Scripture (or Old Testament) and the New Testament, involving two bodies of literature: the Apocrypha of the Old Testament and the Pseudepigrapha of the Old Testament.

Justified: to be acquitted, to be declared righteous or just, as in Romans 4–5.

Millennialism or millenarism: a movement of oppressed and dispossessed people who reject the present moral order because it is too corrupt to be reformed and who look forward to a new heaven/new earth, a new moral order. Jewish apocalypticism is an expression of millennialism.

Parousia: a Greek word meaning "coming," which refers to the second coming of Jesus as the Son of Man or the new Human Being.

Pollution system: a socioreligious structure created by a purity code that divides the world into the two realms of the clean and the unclean.

Purity code: a set of regulations that defines what is pure and clean and therefore holy and acceptable to God, but also what is unclean and defiling and therefore sinful. Specific sacrificial offerings are often prescribed to eliminate the pollution that has been contracted. The Book of Leviticus is a purity code.

Sanhedrin: the Jewish supreme court of antiquity composed of seventy men drawn from the priesthood, the scribes or lawyers, and leading elders of the community.

Similitude: a story that functions like a parable but draws from common experience in order to make a comparison between something well known and something that is unknown or less known. The parable of the mustard seed in Mark 4:30–32 is an example of a similitude.

Sinaitic Syriac: the earliest extant Syriac translation of the New Testament, of which only the Gospels survive, dated between the fourth and fifth centuries. Discovered at St. Catherine's Monastery on Mt. Sinai.

Subjunctive mood: the mood that is employed in Greek for verbs in dependent clauses or verbs that express indefiniteness or contingency.

Syriac Curetonian: an incomplete manuscript of the four Gospels in Syriac that may be a revision of the Sinaitic Syriac.

Syriac Peshitta: the most widely transmitted Syriac translation of the New Testament, which is still used in the Syriac

Orthodox Church. The earliest manuscripts are from the fifth and sixth centuries.

Targum: an Aramaic translation or paraphrase of the Hebrew text of the books of the Old Testament.

Theophany: a manifestation or vision of God, as in Ezekiel 1:26–28.

Torah: a Hebrew word meaning "teaching," which is applied to the five books of Moses and sometimes to the entire Old Testament.

Trajectory: the forward movement of an object, an idea, or a system of thought that is aimed at a specific target or goal.